OPPOSING
VIEWPOINTS®
SERIES

The Taliban

Other Books of Related Interest:

Opposing Viewpoints Series

Extremism

At Issue Series

How Should the U.S. Proceed in Afghanistan?

Current Controversies Series

Iran

"Congress shall make no law … abridging the freedom of speech, or of the press."

First Amendment to the U.S. Constitution

The basic foundation of our democracy is the First Amendment guarantee of freedom of expression. The Opposing Viewpoints Series is dedicated to the concept of this basic freedom and the idea that it is more important to practice it than to enshrine it.

**VIEWPOINTS®
SERIES**

| The Taliban

Noah Berlatsky, Book Editor

GREENHAVEN PRESS
A part of Gale, Cengage Learning

GALE
CENGAGE Learning·

Detroit • New York • San Francisco • New Haven, Conn • Waterville, Maine • London

Christine Nasso, *Publisher*
Elizabeth Des Chenes, *Managing Editor*

© 2011 Greenhaven Press, a part of Gale, Cengage Learning.

Articles in Greenhaven Press anthologies are often edited for length to meet page requirements. In addition, original titles of these works are changed to clearly present the main thesis and to explicitly indicate the author's opinion. Every effort is made to ensure that Greenhaven Press accurately reflects the original intent of the authors. Every effort has been made to trace the owners of copyrighted material.

Cover Image copyright © iStockPhoto.com/Kemter.

LIBRARY OF CONGRESS CATALOGING-IN-PUBLICATION DATA

The Taliban / Noah Berlatsky, book editor.
    p. cm. -- (Opposing viewpoints)
    Includes bibliographical references and index.
    ISBN 978-0-7377-5239-7 (hardcover) -- ISBN 978-0-7377-5240-3 (pbk.)
    1. Taliban--Juvenile literature. 2. Afghanistan--History--1989-2001--Juvenile literature. 3. Afghanistan--History--2001--Juvenile literature. 4. Afghan War, 2001--Juvenile literature. I. Berlatsky, Noah.
    DS371.3.T326 2011
    958.104'6--dc22

                                                                2010030907

Printed in the United States of America
1 2 3 4 5 6 7 14 13 12 11

Contents

Chapter 3: What Is the Taliban's Relationship with Pakistan?

Why Consider Opposing Viewpoints?

> "The only way in which a human being can make some approach to knowing the whole of a subject is by hearing what can be said about it by persons of every variety of opinion and studying all modes in which it can be looked at by every character of mind. No wise man ever acquired his wisdom in any mode but this."
>
> John Stuart Mill

In our media-intensive culture it is not difficult to find differing opinions. Thousands of newspapers and magazines and dozens of radio and television talk shows resound with differing points of view. The difficulty lies in deciding which opinion to agree with and which "experts" seem the most credible. The more inundated we become with differing opinions and claims, the more essential it is to hone critical reading and thinking skills to evaluate these ideas. Opposing Viewpoints books address this problem directly by presenting stimulating debates that can be used to enhance and teach these skills. The varied opinions contained in each book examine many different aspects of a single issue. While examining these conveniently edited opposing views, readers can develop critical thinking skills such as the ability to compare and contrast authors' credibility, facts, argumentation styles, use of persuasive techniques, and other stylistic tools. In short, the Opposing Viewpoints Series is an ideal way to attain the higher-level thinking and reading skills so essential in a culture of diverse and contradictory opinions.

In addition to providing a tool for critical thinking, Opposing Viewpoints books challenge readers to question their own strongly held opinions and assumptions. Most people form their opinions on the basis of upbringing, peer pressure, and personal, cultural, or professional bias. By reading carefully balanced opposing views, readers must directly confront new ideas as well as the opinions of those with whom they disagree. This is not to simplistically argue that everyone who reads opposing views will—or should—change his or her opinion. Instead, the series enhances readers' understanding of their own views by encouraging confrontation with opposing ideas. Careful examination of others' views can lead to the readers' understanding of the logical inconsistencies in their own opinions, perspective on why they hold an opinion, and the consideration of the possibility that their opinion requires further evaluation.

Evaluating Other Opinions

To ensure that this type of examination occurs, Opposing Viewpoints books present all types of opinions. Prominent spokespeople on different sides of each issue as well as well-known professionals from many disciplines challenge the reader. An additional goal of the series is to provide a forum for other, less known, or even unpopular viewpoints. The opinion of an ordinary person who has had to make the decision to cut off life support from a terminally ill relative, for example, may be just as valuable and provide just as much insight as a medical ethicist's professional opinion. The editors have two additional purposes in including these less known views. One, the editors encourage readers to respect others' opinions—even when not enhanced by professional credibility. It is only by reading or listening to and objectively evaluating others' ideas that one can determine whether they are worthy of consideration. Two, the inclusion of such viewpoints encourages the important critical thinking skill of objectively evaluating an author's credentials and bias. This evaluation will illuminate an author's reasons for taking a particular stance on an issue and will aid in readers' evaluation of the author's ideas.

It is our hope that these books will give readers a deeper understanding of the issues debated and an appreciation of the complexity of even seemingly simple issues when good and honest people disagree. This awareness is particularly important in a democratic society such as ours in which people enter into public debate to determine the common good. Those with whom one disagrees should not be regarded as enemies but rather as people whose views deserve careful examination and may shed light on one's own.

Thomas Jefferson once said that "difference of opinion leads to inquiry, and inquiry to truth." Jefferson, a broadly educated man, argued that "if a nation expects to be ignorant and free . . . it expects what never was and never will be." As individuals and as a nation, it is imperative that we consider the opinions of others and examine them with skill and discernment. The Opposing Viewpoints Series is intended to help readers achieve this goal.

David L. Bender and Bruno Leone,
Founders

Introduction

"Watching the Obama administration make nice with Afghan President Hamid Karzai after a bruising fight last month is a little like watching a friend return to a bad marriage with an unreliable spouse."

—Los Angeles Times, *May 11, 2010*

When the United States invaded Afghanistan in 2001 and overthrew the fundamentalist Taliban regime, many hoped that a democratic, pro-Western Afghan government would rule the country. An elected democratic government, it was thought, would have broad support, would be perceived as legitimate, and would therefore be able to control the country and prevent the Taliban from returning to power.

The first presidential elections in Afghanistan were held in 2004. The victor was Hamid Karzai, an Afghan political figure who had been in exile before the American invasion. Though the election was "initially expected to be flawed by violence and vote fraud," according to an article on GlobalSecurity.org, the United Nations found it to be free and fair. Karzai won handily with 55 percent of the vote.

The second Afghan election in August 2009 was more troubled. Karzai ran for re-election; his main opponent was Abdullah Abdullah. The election was marked by low voter turnout, in part because the Taliban and other militants threatened to target polling places and kill voters. These threats were borne out—there were several bombing attacks on polling centers. "In the southern city of Kandahar insurgents hanged two people because their fingers were marked with the ink showing they had voted," according to Haroon Siddique writing in an August 20, 2009, *Guardian* article. There were also rocket attacks and other violence. Siddique noted that in the southern city of Kandahar in the middle of Taliban territory, voting was down 40 percent from 2004, with women voters particularly likely to stay home.

Even more worrisome than the violence and low turnout was endemic fraud. Carlotta Gall noted in an August 22, 2009, *New York Times* article that there were "widespread accounts of ballot-box stuffing, a lack of impartiality among election workers and voters casting ballots for others." Peter W. Galbraith, who was part of the United Nations team overseeing the election, wrote in *Time* on October 19, 2009, "In some provinces, many more votes were counted than were cast. E.U. [European Union] election monitors characterize 1.5 million votes as suspect, which would include up to one-third of the votes cast for incumbent President Hamid Karzai."

The election results showed Karzai received 54.6 percent of the vote, enough for him to win outright. However, independent election officials found that a large number of his votes were fraudulent, and determined that he had actually received closer to 46 percent of the vote. The lower total required a run-off election between Karzai and his main challenger, Abdullah. Under pressure from Western allies, Karzai agreed to the run-off, and it was scheduled to be held in November 2009. However, it was unclear how the second round would be any less fraudulent than the first. Galbraith claimed in a November 1, 2009, article in the *Los Angeles Times* that "it has become clear that Karzai and his allies are determined to win the second round by any means possible, regardless of the cost to the country or the international military effort." Many also feared that there would be more insurgent violence and that turnout would be even lower than in the first round.

Eventually, less than a week before the November 7 election, Abdullah Abdullah announced he was dropping out of the voting because "his demands for ensuring a fraud-free election had not been met," according to a November 1, 2009, *BBC News* report. Abdullah's decision to pull out left "an election process with battered credibility and a nominal victor, Mr Karzai, whose supporters have already been convicted of a spectacular million vote fraud in the first round of voting," according to Tom Coughlan writing in the *Times* of London on November 1, 2009.

The fraudulent election results seriously complicated the battle against the Taliban, and Karzai resented U.S. accusations. In a series of angry statements, he accused the West of perpetrating fraud in the elections, and he threatened to ally with the Taliban if the United States continued to pressure him. For its part, "the Obama administration still doesn't trust Karzai" and officials say his "lack of credibility among his people poses the biggest threat to U.S. success against the Taliban," according to Elise Labott writing in a May 13, 2010, essay on CNN.com. The Taliban insurgency thrives on instability and dissatisfaction, both of which are increased when the government is widely seen by the Afghan people as illegitimate.

Opposing Viewpoints: The Taliban examines other challenges and difficulties facing the United States, Afghanistan, and the world in confronting the Taliban. In the chapters— "Who Are the Taliban?" "How Should the United States Deal with the Taliban?" "What Is the Taliban's Relationship with Pakistan?" and "What Is the Taliban's Relationship with Other Nations?"—viewpoint authors provide different perspectives on how and whether the Taliban can be defeated in Afghanistan and Central Asia.

OPPOSING
VIEWPOINTS®
SERIES

CHAPTER 1

Who Are the Taliban?

Chapter Preface

The Taliban is the name given to a militant Islamic fundamentalist movement in Afghanistan. The leader of the Afghan Taliban is Mohammad Omar, also called Mullah Omar.

Omar has been the head of the Taliban for more than fifteen years, and was the ruler of Afghanistan itself from 1996 to 2001. Yet little is known about him. There are no definite photos of him, and "no Western journalist has ever met" him, according to a *BBC News* profile published on September 18, 2001. He has, however, been interviewed by journalists from the Muslim world.

Omar is reported to have been born in the 1950s or early 1960s, either in the central Afghan province of Uruzgan or in the southern province of Kandahar. He may have studied in Islamic schools in Pakistan. Then, in 1979, the Soviet Union invaded Afghanistan. Like many fundamentalist Afghans, Omar joined the militant Islamic resistance. He is supposed to have "lost his eyes fighting the Soviets," according to a biography on *Afghanistan Online*, published in 1997 and updated in 2007.

Following the Soviet defeat and withdrawal in the late 1980s, Omar founded a religious school, or madrassah. As Afghanistan descended into civil war, Omar determined to unify and stabilize the country. Starting with less than 50 armed students, he eventually did just that. Omar's growing army, called the Taliban, gained effective control of Afghanistan in 1996, imposing strict religious laws and restrictions, especially on women. In the same year, Omar took the title "Amirul Momineen," or "Defender of the Faithful." That is "a ranking in Islam nearly second to the Prophet," and had not been claimed by any Muslim in almost 1,500 years, according to Robert Marquand writing in the *Christian Science Monitor* on October 10, 2001.

Marquand also reported that, at first, Omar was not interested in exporting Muslim holy war, or jihad, outside of Afghanistan. However, Omar eventually seems to have become closer to Osama bin Laden, the leader of the al Qaeda terrorist network that launched repeated attacks on Western targets. After the successful September 11, 2001, al Qaeda terrorist attacks on American soil, Omar and the Taliban leadership refused to turn bin Laden over to American authorities. In an effort to capture bin Laden, the United States then invaded Afghanistan and overthrew the Taliban regime. Omar was reportedly forced to flee on a motorbike.

Many thought that would be the end of Mullah Omar. But instead, Omar's Taliban regrouped to stage an extended, bitter, and often successful insurgency campaign against the American-supported Afghan government. Bruce Riedel, a former Central Intelligence Agency (CIA) agent, was quoted in an October 11, 2009, *New York Times* article as stating of Omar, "He's a semiliterate individual who has met with no more than a handful of non-Muslims in his entire life. And he's staged one of the most remarkable military comebacks in modern history."

The *New York Times* story, written by Scott Shane, notes that it is unclear whether the military successes of the Taliban are due to Omar's particular genius. Indeed, Omar may be at this point mostly a figurehead, with decisions made by his deputies, perhaps with advice from sympathetic elements in Pakistan's intelligence service or al Qaeda. Whatever Omar's exact role is, however, after a decade and a half he remains a figure of major importance to Afghanistan's future.

The viewpoints in this chapter examine the exact make-up of the Taliban, their relationship with al Qaeda, and their goals and policies.

> *"Almost all areas that are either Taliban-controlled or Taliban-influenced, are Pashtun."*

The Taliban Are a Pashtun Nationalist Movement

Michael J. Totten

Michael J. Totten is a journalist and award-winning blogger whose work has appeared in The New York Times, The Wall Street Journal, The Jerusalem Post, *and other publications. In the following viewpoint, he says that the Taliban are an expression of nationalist sentiment by an ethnic group called the Pashtuns. Most Pashtuns are concentrated along the border between Afghanistan and Pakistan, and in this region, Totten says, the Taliban are strong. Totten argues, however, that the Taliban will have trouble moving beyond Pashtun areas, because other ethnic groups will not want to be subjugated by a Pashtun movement.*

As you read, consider the following questions:

1. In addition to being an expression of Pashtun nationalism, how else does Totten describe the Taliban?

2. According to Totten, what ethnic group primarily makes up the Northern Alliance?

3. Why has al Qaeda in Iraq had little effect on the Kurdish parts of the country, according to Totten?

Pakistan is looking more dangerous and precarious by the
week. The only Muslim country in the world with an ar-
senal of nuclear weapons is now threatened by a ferocious and
rapidly expanding Taliban insurgency. The most retrograde Islamist army on earth has conquered territory just a few hours'
drive from the capital. Though this discouraging outcome
wasn't inevitable, it was at least likely. As Robert Kaplan
pointed out in an insightful essay in the current issue of Foreign Policy magazine, "the Taliban constitute merely the latest
incarnation of Pashtun [an ethic group; many of the Taliban
are Pashtuns] nationalism." And ethnic Pashtuns live on both
sides of the Afghanistan-Pakistan border. "Indeed," Kaplan
adds, "much of the fighting in Afghanistan today occurs in
Pashtunistan: southern and eastern Afghanistan and the tribal
areas of Pakistan."

The Taliban in Pashtunistan

Take a look at two maps [not shown]. The first shows the
geographic breakdown of Pakistan's patchwork of ethnicities.
You'll notice that ethnic Pashtuns live in the notoriously back-
ward and violent northwestern frontier provinces. Their region extends deep into Afghanistan and covers the southeast-
ern part of that country. These two regions—which are
actually a single region with a somewhat arbitrary national
border between them—are where most Taliban activity has
been concentrated since the United States destroyed their regime in Afghanistan [when the United States invaded in 2001].
A second map shows the breakdown of areas in Pakistan currently under Taliban control. You'll see, when you compare the
maps carefully, that almost all areas that are either Taliban-
controlled or Taliban-influenced, are Pashtun.

The Taliban are more than an expression of Pashtun nationalism, of course. They represent a reactionary movement

that idealizes the simplicity and extreme conservatism of 7th century Islam. By burnishing this ideology, the Taliban is able, absurdly, to attract support beyond its Pashtun base.

The ethnic component, though, is a formidable one. It all but guaranteed a certain degree of success by the Taliban in all of "Pashtunistan," in Pakistan as well as in Afghanistan. Yet all the while, the ethnic map imposes constraints, if not limits, on how far the Taliban can expand.

They were able to seize power in most of Afghanistan before 2001, although the "Northern Alliance" [a group of Afghans who fought the Taliban];—made up primarily of ethnic Tajiks—managed to hold out until Americans arrived and smashed the regime in Kabul [the capital of Afghanistan]. Since then, the Taliban have had a harder time operating outside "Pashtunistan." "The north of Afghanistan," Kaplan writes, "beyond the Hindu Kush [a mountain range on the Pakistan/Afghanistan border], has seen less fighting and is in the midst of reconstruction and the forging of closer links to the former Soviet republics in Central Asia, inhabited by the same ethnic groups that populate northern Afghanistan."

Ethnic Limits

The Taliban have been able to operate in some areas outside their ethnic perimeter, even so. The maps demonstrate that, as well. "Pashtunistan" is their platform. They aren't prisoners of their own demographics. They can seize territory beyond their base, but it's harder.

Armed radical groups in the Middle East run up against similar constraints and limits. Al Qaeda [a terrorist group] in Iraq has never been able to hold territory outside Sunni Arab areas. They have been able to terrorize Shia Arab neighborhoods in Baghdad [the capital of Iraq], but they can hardly do that much in the Kurdish parts of the country, even though

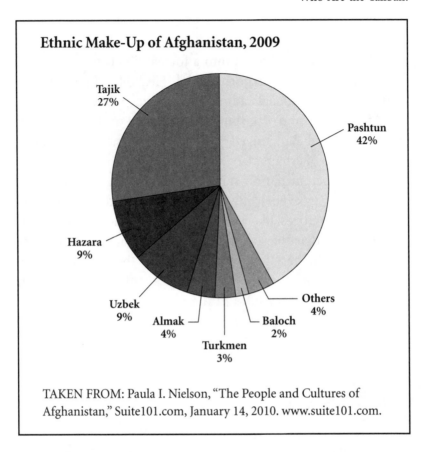

Ethnic Make-Up of Afghanistan, 2009

Tajik
27%

Pashtun
42%

Hazara
9%

Uzbek
9%

Almak
4%

Turkmen
3%

Baloch
2%

Others
4%

TAKEN FROM: Paula I. Nielson, "The People and Cultures of Afghanistan," Suite101.com, January 14, 2010. www.suite101.com.

most Iraqi Kurds also are Sunnis.[1] Iraq's sectarian boundaries are difficult to breach, but the ethnic boundaries are like walls.

Hezbollah [a Shia Islamist paramilitary organization] in Lebanon has a similar problem. Hardly anyone who isn't a Shia sincerely supports them or their program. A few Sunnis and Druze [a religion similar to Islam], and a larger number of Christians, are willing to tolerate a Shia Islamist militia as a powerful electoral coalition partner for tactical reasons, but they will never submit to a Shia theocracy or the

1. Sunni and Shia are branches of Islam. The Kurds are a distinct ethnic group that often has been at odds with the majority Arab population of Iraq.

transformation of Lebanon into a formal jihad state or a satellite of Iran [which is majority Shia]. Hezbollah knows it, too, and many of its officials admit as much in public.

Afghanistan and Pakistan, like Lebanon and Iraq, are hypercomplicated Balkanized patchwork states. They're inherently unstable. Perhaps they always will be if they don't subdivide into coherent nation-states as most of Yugoslavia did. It's hard to predict events anywhere in the world, and it's even harder in countries like these. One thing, though, is all but certain. Now that the Taliban have consolidated power in Pashtunistan, whether they seize control of the capital and the rest of the country or not, they will face stiffer resistance from here on out than they have in the past.

"*Afghan officials say an alliance of these three groups [the Taliban, al Qaeda, and Hizb-i Islami] may present the greatest security challenge to the fragile transitional government.*"

The Taliban Are Part of Global Jihadism and Allied with al Qaeda

Scott Baldauf and Owais Tohid

Scott Baldauf is a staff writer and frequent contributor to the Christian Science Monitor. *Owais Tohid is a journalist from Pakistan and a correspondent for the* Christian Science Monitor. *In the following article, the authors discuss the regrouping of the terrorist organization al Qaeda with the Taliban and the radical Islamist party Hizb-i Islami. While signs of the regrouping have been limited, Afghan officials believe that an alliance between these groups would present a large security challenge.*

As you read, consider the following questions:

    1. Who is Sana Hamid?

Scott Baldauf and Owais Tohid, "A Triangle of Militants Regroups in Afghanistan; Intelligence Officials Say Al Qaeda and Taliban Are Tied to a Radical Islamist Party," *Christian Science Monitor*, April 9, 2003. Reproduced by permission from *Christian Science Monitor*. www.csmonitor.com.

2. According to the article, what has caused most Hizb-i Islami leaders to go underground?

3. As stated in the article, are the rumors of an alliance between Hizb-i Islami, Taliban, and al Qaeda confirmed?

Sana Hamid has come to Pakistan to recruit a few good terrorists.

Not just anyone will do. There are plenty of people in this part of Pakistan who would love to fight American forces in Afghanistan. But Mr. Hamid and his Afghan guerrilla leader, Gulbuddin Hekmatyar, need people with skills that will mesh with their allies—the Taliban and Al Qaeda.

"We are trying to regroup into a force like we were during Afghan Jihad (the Soviet-Afghan war)," says Hamid, a former information official for his party, the Hizb-i Islami. He spoke to the [*Christian Science*] *Monitor* on condition that neither his location nor his real name would be disclosed.

Taliban and Al Qaeda Regroup

For months, Afghan and US intelligence officials have warned about a regrouping of Al Qaeda and the Taliban on both sides of the porous Afghan-Pakistani border. More ominous still for the war in Afghanistan is the reported alliance of America's enemies with old friends from the Soviet war, namely the radical Islamist party Hizb-i Islami [Hizb]. Some leaflets signed by Hizb and Taliban leaders have even called on Muslims to join an all-out jihad or holy struggle against American forces timed to the beginning of America's war in Iraq.

"We do not need military training, as even an eight- and 10-year old boy knows how to use a Kalashnikov [assault rifle]," Hamid says. "We have suicide squads of Al Qaeda. They are like walking bombs, and they are our biggest weapons against Americans in Afghanistan."

While signs of this regrouping are mostly limited to a scattering of printed leaflets and a few fiery speeches in local mosques Afghan officials say an alliance of these three groups may present the greatest security challenge to the fragile transitional government of Afghan President Hamid Karzai and to the American forces who remain behind to keep the peace.

"There is a slow return of the evil triangle, made up of the Taliban, Al Qaeda, and Hizb-i Islami, and at the top of this triangle is the man who is the shrewdest, and that is Hekmatyar," says Masood Khalili, the Afghan ambassador to India in New Delhi. "These elements think that America will be distracted by the war in Iraq, and that the US will not stay in Afghanistan. This is not true, I think. But if we do lose the Afghanistan battle, we will lose the war against the terrorists."

While the activities of Hizb are known in just about every mosque or bazaar along the Afghan border, most Hizb supporters remain quite out of sight. And most prominent Hizb leaders have gone underground as a result of a Pakistani crackdown on radical Islamist groups.

One top leader, Qutbuddin Hilal, a former second in command under Mr. Hekmatyar, now lives under virtual house arrest in Hayatabad, a suburb of Peshawar. Pakistani authorities say the detention is for Mr. Hilal's protection: Hilal recently broke with Hekmatyar to back the Karzai government.

But the Hizb public presence is not completely erased.

Hizb Members

In the massive Shamshatoo refugee camp, just 15 miles from Peshawar, in a guardhouse that bears the sign "Hizb-i Islami Afghanistan Education Committee," some Hizb members politely share their ambivalence toward the new Karzai government, the US troops, and about the rumors of their own party's newly announced jihad.

"Yes, we've heard about this jihad, but we don't know what is really happening in Afghanistan," says Noor Mohammad, head of the Hizb guards at Shamshatoo camp. "What we know we have read in the newspapers."

"Right now we don't know where [Hekmatyar] is, and he doesn't know where we are," says Noor Mohammad, coyly. "If Hekmatyar announces good policies, we will welcome him. But whosoever continues any of the old mistakes, whether he's Hekmatyar or Karzai, we will fight him."

Sultan Mehmud, editor of *Shahadaat*, a pro-Hizb-i-Islami newspaper in Peshawar, says he's not sure how much of the talk of Hizb regrouping is either propaganda by Afghan authorities or wishful thinking by Hizb itself. Still, he concedes there is substantial anger among Afghans and Afghan refugees.

"If the government left all those Taliban people alone, they would shave their beards and come back to enjoy the peace," says Mr. Mehmud. "But now the Americans are coming to your homes, capturing your brothers, humiliating your sister, and saying 'You are Taliban.' By their own hands, they are forcing the Taliban to regroup again. If America had one opponent before, they have two or three opponents now."

Loss of Faith in Karzai Government

Like most ethnic Pashtuns, who make up the largest ethnic group in Afghanistan as well as a significant minority in Pakistan, Hamid says he has lost faith in the Karzai government.

Part of this loss of faith is based on a desire to impose an Islamic-style government in Afghanistan, instead of a democracy, and also on a popular Pashtun belief that Karzai relies too heavily on the power of the ethnic Tajik minority. The Tajiks control the Northern Alliance, a private army which helped US forces to oust the Taliban regime.

"Everybody has a consensus in Afghanistan that the job of the foreign forces is finished and the Northern Alliance cannot rule Afghanistan," Hamid says.

Traveling in a day from his home base in the Afghan province of Laghman, Hamid easily entered Pakistan under an assumed name, using the legal border crossing of Torkham in the famed Khyber Pass.

He confirms rumors that Hizb, Taliban, and Al Qaeda leaders have formed an alliance of their own, in which each group operates in areas where their strength is greatest. Hizb's strength is greatest in the Afghan provinces of Konar, Nangrahar, Laghman, Logar, Paktia, and Khost.

The Taliban's strength is greatest in Kandahar, Helmand, Zabol, Uruzgan, and Nimroz. Al Qaeda's positions are more fluid, filling in gaps and constantly moving.

Yet Hamid admits that the uprising still has its problems to confront. "We do have difficulties," he says. "The biggest hurdle is to counter the B-52s that fire at us and all we can do is watch helplessly. That is why we are targeting the US bases or ambushing their convoys."

> "Local commanders often set their own policies and initiate attacks without direct orders from the leadership. The result is a slippery movement that morphs from district to district."

The Taliban Cannot Be Categorized Easily as Any One Movement

Anand Gopal

Anand Gopal is an Afghanistan-based journalist who has written for The Wall Street Journal, Christian Science Monitor, *and other publications. In the following viewpoint, he argues that the term "the Taliban" actually refers to a number of different groups. Gopal says these groups are not centrally organized and have different goals and methods, but they are united by opposition to the occupation. Gopal argues that the Taliban is not closely allied with al Qaeda, and that its popularity primarily is due to the failure of Western forces to provide security, and the Taliban's promise to do so.*

As you read, consider the following questions:

1. How much does Gopal say that the insurgents pay conscripted fighters per month, and how does this compare with a typical police salary?
2. Who is Mullah Brehadar?
3. What is Hizb-i-Islami?

If there is an exact location marking the West's failures in Afghanistan, it is the modest police checkpoint that sits on the main highway twenty minutes south of Kabul [Afghanistan's capital]. The post signals the edge of the capital, a city of spectacular tension, of blast walls and standstill traffic. Beyond this point, Kabul's gritty, low-slung buildings and narrow streets give way to a vast plain of serene farmland, hemmed in by sandy mountains. In this valley in Logar province, the American-backed government of Afghanistan no longer exists [as of December 2008].

The Taliban in Control

Instead of government officials, men in muddied black turbans with assault rifles slung over their shoulders patrol the highway, checking for thieves and "spies." The charred carcass of a tanker, meant to deliver fuel to international forces farther south, sits belly-up on the roadside. The police say they don't dare enter these districts, especially at night, when the guerrillas rule the roads. In some parts of the country's south and east, these insurgents have even set up their own government, which they call the Islamic Emirate of Afghanistan, the name of the former Taliban government [which controlled Afghanistan from 1996 to 2001]. They mete out justice in makeshift Sharia [Islamic law] courts. They settle land disputes between villagers. They dictate the curriculum in schools.

Just three years ago [2005], the central government still controlled the provinces near Kabul. But years of mismanagement, rampant criminality and mounting civilian casualties inflicted by Western forces have led to a spectacular resurgence of the Taliban and related groups. According to Acbar, an umbrella organization representing more than 100 aid agencies, insurgent attacks have increased by 50 percent over the past year. Foreign soldiers are now dying at a higher rate here than in Iraq.

The worsening disaster is prompting the Afghan government of President Hamid Karzai and international players to speak openly of negotiations with sections of the insurgency. But who exactly are the Afghan insurgents? Every suicide attack and kidnapping is usually attributed to "the Taliban." In reality, however, the insurgency is far from monolithic. There are the shadowy, kohl-eyed mullahs and head-bobbing religious students, of course, but there are also erudite university students, veteran anti-Soviet commanders and poor, illiterate farmers. The movement is a mélange of nationalists, Islamists and bandits that fall uneasily into three or four main factions and many subfactions. The factions have competing commanders with differing ideologies and strategies, who nonetheless agree on one essential goal: kicking out the foreigners.

The Loss of Afghanistan

It wasn't always this way. When US-led forces toppled the Taliban government in November 2001, Afghans celebrated the downfall of a reviled and discredited regime. "We felt like dancing in the streets," one Kabuli told me. As US-backed forces marched into Kabul, remnants of the old Taliban regime split into three groups. The first, including many Kabul-based bureaucrats and functionaries, simply surrendered to the Americans; some even joined the Karzai government. The second, comprising the movement's senior leadership, including "Commander of the Faithful" Mullah Omar, fled across the border into Pakistan, where they remain to this day. The third and largest group—foot soldiers, local commanders and provincial officials—quietly melted into the landscape, returning to their villages to wait and see which way the wind would blow.

Meanwhile, the country was quickly being carved up by warlords and criminals. On the brand-new highway connecting Kabul to Kandahar and Herat, built with millions of Washington's [U.S.] dollars, well-organized groups of bandits would regularly terrorize travelers. Last year [2007] "thirty, maybe fifty criminals, some in police uniforms, stopped our bus and shot [out] our windows," Muhammadullah, the owner of a bus company that regularly uses the route, told me. "They searched our vehicle and stole everything from everyone." Criminal syndicates, often with government connections, organized kidnapping sprees in urban centers. Often, those few who were caught would simply be released after the right palms were greased.

Into this landscape of violence and criminality rode the Taliban, promising law and order—just as they did when they first formed in the mid-1990s, when they were welcomed by many Afghans as relief from the rapacious post-Soviet warlords.[1] Within two years after the 2001 invasion, the exiled leadership, based in Quetta, Pakistan, began reactivating networks of fighters who had blended into Afghan villages. They resurrected relationships with Pashtun tribes. (The insurgents, historically a predominantly Pashtun movement and mostly concentrated in the country's south and east, still have very little influence among other minority ethnic groups like the Tajiks, Uzbeks and Hezaras.) With funds from wealthy Arab donors and training from ISI [Inter-Services Intelligence], the Pakistani intelligence apparatus, they were able to bring weapons and expertise into Pashtun villages.

In one village after another, the Taliban drove out the remaining minority of government sympathizers through intimidation and assassination. Then they won over the

1. The Soviet Union tried to occupy Afghanistan in the 1980s; they were driven out by militant Islamic groups. When the Soviets left, there was a struggle for power, which the Taliban won.

majority with promises of security and efficiency. They implemented a harsh version of Sharia law, cutting off the hands of thieves and shooting adulterers. They were brutal, but they were also incorruptible. Justice no longer went to the highest bidder. "There's no crime anymore, unlike before," said Abdul Halim, who lives in a district under Taliban control.

The insurgents conscripted fighters from the villages they operated in, often paying $200 a month—more than double the typical police salary. They adjudicated disputes between tribes and between landowners. They protected poppy [used to create opium] fields from the eradication attempts of the central government and foreign armies—a move that won the support of poor farmers whose only stable income came from poppy cultivation. The areas under insurgent control were consigned to having neither reconstruction nor social services, but for rural villagers who had seen much foreign intervention and little economic progress under the Karzai government, this was hardly new.

At the same time, the Taliban's ideology began to transform. "We are fighting to free our country from foreign domination," Taliban spokesman Qari Yousef Ahmadi told me over the phone. "The Indians fought for their independence against the British. Even the Americans once waged an insurgency to free their own country." This emerging nationalistic streak appeals to Pashtun villagers, who have grown weary of the American and NATO [North Atlantic Treaty Organization] presence.

The Taliban Become More Pragmatic

The insurgents are also fighting to install a version of Sharia law. Nonetheless, the famously puritanical guerrillas have moderated some of their most extreme doctrines, at least in principle. Last year, for instance, Mullah Omar issued an edict declaring music and parties—banned in the Taliban's previous incarnation—permissible. Some commanders have even started accepting the idea of girls' education. Certain hardline leaders such as the one-legged Mullah Dadullah, a man of legendary brutality whose beheading binges reportedly proved too much even for Mullah Omar, were killed by international forces.

At the same time, a more pragmatic leadership started taking the reins. American intelligence officials believe day-to-day leadership of the movement is now in the hands of the politically savvy Mullah Brehadar, while Mullah Omar retains a largely figurehead position. Brehadar may be behind the push to moderate the movement's message in order to win support. Even at the local level, some Taliban officials are tempering their older policies in order to win local hearts and minds. Three months ago in a district in Ghazni province, for instance, the insurgents ordered all schools closed. Tribal elders appealed to the Taliban's ruling religious council in the area; the religious judges reversed the decision and reopened the schools.

However, not all field commanders follow the central injunctions. In many Taliban-controlled districts such amusements as music and parties are still outlawed, which points to the movement's decentralized nature. Local commanders often set their own policies and initiate attacks without direct orders from the leadership. The result is a slippery movement that morphs from district to district. In some Taliban-controlled districts of Ghazni province, an Afghan caught working for a nongovernmental organization [NGO] would meet certain death. In parts of neighboring Wardak province, however, where the insurgents are said to be more educated and understand the need for development, local NGOs can function with the guerrillas' permission.

Hizb-i-Islami

Never short of guns and guerrillas, Afghanistan has proven fertile ground for a host of insurgent groups in addition to the Taliban.

Naqibullah, a student with a sparse beard who spoke in soft, measured tones, was not quite 30 when we met. We were parked in the back seat of a dusty Corolla on a pockmarked road near Kabul University, where he studied medicine. Naqibullah (his nom de guerre [pseudonym]) and his friends at the university are members of Hizb-i-Islami, an insurgent group led by warlord Gulbuddin Hekmatyar and allied with the Taliban. Naqibullah's circle of friends meet regularly in the university's dorms, discussing politics and watching DVDs of recent attacks. Over the past year his circle has shrunk: Sadiq was arrested while attempting a suicide bombing. Wasim was killed when he tried to assemble a bomb at home. Fouad killed himself in a successful suicide attack on a US base. "The Americans have their B-52s," Naqibullah explained. "Suicide attacks are our versions of B-52s." Like his friends, Naqibullah had considered becoming a B-52. "But it would kill too many civilians," he told me. Besides, he had plans to use his education. He said, "I want to teach the uneducated Taliban."

For years Hizb-i-Islami fighters have had a reputation for being more educated and worldly than their Taliban counterparts, who are often illiterate farmers. Their leader, [Gulbuddin] Hekmatyar, studied engineering at Kabul University in the 1970s, where he made a name for himself by hurling acid in the faces of unveiled women. Hekmatyar established Hizb-i-Islami to counter growing Soviet influence, and in the 1980s his organization became one of the most extreme fundamentalist parties as well as the leading mujahedeen [Islamic fighter] group fighting the Soviet occupation. Ruthless, powerful and anti-Communist, Hekmatyar proved a capable ally for

Washington, which, along with the Saudis, funneled billions of dollars and tons of weapons through the Pakistani ISI to his forces.

After the Soviet withdrawal, Hekmatyar and the other mujahedeen commanders turned their guns on one another, unleashing a devastating civil war from which Kabul, in particular, has yet to recover. One-legged Afghans, crippled by Hekmatyar's rockets, still roam the city's streets. However, he was unable to capture the capital, and his Pakistani backers eventually abandoned him for a new, even more extreme Islamist force rising in the south: the Taliban.

Most Hizb-i-Islami commanders defected to the Taliban, and Hekmatyar fled in disgrace to Iran, losing much of his support in the process. He remained in such low standing that he was among the few warlords not offered a place in the US-backed government that formed after 2001. This, after a fashion, was his good luck. When that government faltered, he found himself thrust back into the role of insurgent leader, and, playing on local frustrations in Pashtun communities just as the Taliban have done, he slowly resurrected Hizb-i-Islami.

Today the group is one of the fastest-growing insurgent outfits in the country, according to Antonio Giustozzi, Afghan insurgency expert at the London School of Economics. Hizb-i-Islami maintains a strong presence in the provinces near Kabul and in Pashtun pockets in the country's north and northeast. It assisted in a complex assassination attempt on President Karzai this past spring [2008] and was behind a high-profile ambush that killed ten NATO soldiers last summer. Its guerrillas fight under the Taliban banner, although independently and with a separate command structure. Like the Taliban, its leaders see their task as restoring Afghan sovereignty as well as establishing an Islamic state in Afghanistan. Naqibullah explained, "The US installed a puppet regime here. It was an affront to Islam, an injustice that all Afghans should rise up against."

The independent Islamic state that Hizb-i-Islami is fighting for would undoubtedly have Hekmatyar, not Mullah Omar, in command. But as during the anti-Soviet jihad, the settling of scores is largely being left to the future.

Living in a World of War

Blowback abounds in Afghanistan. Erstwhile CIA [Central Intelligence Agency] hand Jalaluddin Haqqani heads yet a third insurgent network, this one based in the eastern border regions. During the anti-Soviet war, the United States gave Haqqani, now considered by many to be Washington's most redoubtable foe, millions of dollars, antiaircraft missiles and even tanks. Washington was so enamored of him that former Congressman Charlie Wilson once called him "goodness personified."

Haqqani was an early advocate of the "Afghan Arabs," who in the 1980s flocked to Pakistan to join the jihad against the Soviet Union. He ran training camps for them and later developed close ties to Al Qaeda [a terrorist group], which developed out of the Afghan Arab networks toward the end of the anti-Soviet war. After 9/11 [the September 11, 2001, terrorist attacks on the United States] the United States tried desperately to bring him over to its side, but Haqqani said he couldn't countenance a foreign presence on Afghan soil and once again took up arms, aided by his longtime benefactors in ISI. He is said to have introduced suicide bombing to Afghanistan, a tactic unheard of here before 2001. Western intelligence officials pin the blame for most of the spectacular attacks in recent memory—a massive car bomb that ripped apart the Indian embassy in July [2008], for example—on the Haqqani network, not the Taliban.

The Haqqanis command the lion's share of foreign fighters operating in the country and tend to be even more extreme than their Taliban counterparts. Unlike most of the Taliban and Hizb-i-Islami, elements of the Haqqani network cooperate closely with Al Qaeda. Moreover, foreigners associated with the "Pakistani Taliban"—a completely separate organization that is at war with the Pakistani government—and various Pakistani guerrilla groups that were once active in Kashmir [a region disputed by India and Pakistan] also filter across the border into Afghanistan, adding to a mix that has produced what one Western intelligence official calls a "rainbow coalition" that fights US troops. The foreign connection comes naturally, as the leadership of the three main wings of the insurgency is believed to be based across the border in Pakistan, and all insurgent groups are flush with funds from wealthy Arab donors and benefit from ISI training.

But the Afghan rebellion is mostly a homegrown affair. Foreign fighters, especially Al Qaeda, have little ideological influence on most of the insurgency, and Afghans keep their distance from such outsiders. "Sometimes groups of foreigners speaking different languages walk past," Ghazni resident Fazel Wali recalled. "We never talk to them, and they don't talk to us."

Al Qaeda's vision of global jihad doesn't resonate in the rugged highlands and windswept deserts of southern Afghanistan. Instead, the major concern throughout much of the country is intensely local: personal safety. In a world of endless war, with a predatory government, roving bandits and Hellfire missiles, support goes to those who can bring security. In recent months, one of the most dangerous activities in Afghanistan has also been one of its most celebratory: the large, festive wedding parties that Afghans love so much. American forces bombed such a party in July, killing forty-seven. Then, in November, warplanes hit another wedding party, killing around forty. A couple of weeks later they hit an engagement party, killing three.

"We are starting to think that we shouldn't go out in large numbers or have public weddings," Ghazni resident Abdullah Wali told me. Wali lives in a district of Ghazni where the insurgents have outlawed music and dance at such wedding parties. It's an austere life, but that doesn't stop Wali from wanting the Taliban back in power. Bland weddings, it seems, are better than no weddings at all.

| "Basically, people are dying where poppies are thriving."

The Taliban Are Funded by Money from Narcotics

Hayder Mili

Hayder Mili is a United Nations expert specializing in terrorism and security issues in Central Asia and the Caucasus. In the following viewpoint, he argues that poppy production funds Taliban operations, and that it is central to the insurgency's success in Afghanistan. He suggests that U.S.-led coalition forces need to exploit Muslim antipathy to controlled substances, compensate poppy farmers, and adapt counter-narcotics efforts based on the fact that poppy growth and insurgent power are both concentrated in southern Afghanistan. He concludes that counter-narcotics efforts are vital if the Taliban are to be defeated.

As you read, consider the following questions:

1. According to Mili, how much opium was produced in 2006 in Afghanistan, and how much income did it generate?

2. What does Mili say that young locals hired by the Taliban are generally employed to do?

Hayder Mili, "Afghanistan's Drug Trade and How It Funds Taliban Operations," *Terrorism Monitor*, vol. 5, May 10, 2007. Copyright © 2007 The Jamestown Foundation. Reproduced by permission.

3. According to Mili, the United Nations Office on Drugs and Crime found that more than a third of farmers who had not planted poppies in Afghanistan chose not to do so for what reason?

The opium economy in Afghanistan is a key component of the counter-insurgency campaign, yet remains one of the most difficult issues to tackle. It is a critical problem facing international efforts to create a functional government in Kabul [the Afghan capital] that can prosecute counter-terrorism on its own territory. A successful counter-narcotics intervention would have the added benefit of undermining an important terrorist funding source in arenas as diverse as Chechnya [a Russian province that has been the location of an independence movement and terrorist activity], Xinjiang [a region in China that has been the site of ethnic tensions] and Central Asia. While coalition and Afghan officials regularly acknowledge the power that the narco-economy has over their ambitions, it has proven exceptionally challenging to turn this into a national strategy that incorporates counter-narcotics into counter-insurgency and provides the resources for its execution.

Opium Boom

According to the United Nations Office on Drugs and Crime (UNODC), opium production had a boom year in 2006, rising to 6,100 metric tons. This marked a 49% increase over 2005, yielding an estimated $755 million to farmers on the basis of a slightly decreased farm-gate price [the price at the farm] of $125 per kilogram of dry opium. With the national government's revenues at less than $350 million for 2006, the opium economy is a formidable financial power base beyond the state's control. Good weather conditions are expected in 2007, suggesting another huge harvest.

Any national counter-narcotics strategy for Afghanistan must begin with a preface noting the geographical variations of the country. In 2006, the southern province of Helmand accounted for 46% of Afghanistan's opium production. To the east of Helmand, Kandahar produced eight percent. In other words, the majority of Afghanistan's opium economy is built on production in two southern provinces. Of the remainder, 25% is produced in the northern belt close to the borders with Tajikistan, Uzbekistan and Turkmenistan, with lighter concentrations in the eastern and western provinces. Based on the UNODC's observations of recent opium planting, southern pre-eminence is likely to intensify further in 2007. The distribution of production correlates strongly with areas of ongoing insurgency/terrorism and coalition fatalities. Using NATO's [North Atlantic Treaty Organization] divisions of Afghanistan, Regional Command South, which includes Helmand and Kandahar provinces, is where 62% of the country's opium is produced and where the coalition [U.S. and allied forces] has suffered close to two-thirds of its combat deaths. Basically, people are dying where poppies are thriving.

The difference between the relatively calm north and west and the militarized south and east should be reflected in approaches to counter-narcotics. Opium is undoubtedly a governance problem across the country. In the south and east, however, it is also strongly related to the Kabul government's most immediate existential threat—the Taliban-led insurgency—as well as to the funding of 139 suicide attacks in 2006.

Poppy Money Fuels the Insurgency

Out of Afghanistan's total opium production, 21% is trafficked northward through Central Asia. Around 31% travels directly to Iran, which has suffered considerable human and financial costs in responding to both the direct drug traffic and the substantial opiate shipments arriving via Pakistan. The remaining majority of opiates leave Afghanistan across its 2,430 kilometer border with Pakistan. Harsh terrain, corruption and insecurity make it difficult or impossible to interdict opiate flows in most places.

In practice, it is challenging to differentiate between criminality, farmers' economic needs, insurgency fundraising and state complicity. Separating these factors conceptually, however, helps to formulate effective counter-insurgency tactics, highlighting the interactions between the drug trade and the Taliban. According to officials from the United Nations who interviewed Afghan law enforcement and coalition agencies in 2007, a symbiosis between the opiate trade and the Taliban continues, to the extent that some Taliban units simultaneously organize drug production and insurgent activities. In some regions, there has been a methodical process of fighting for territory while establishing relationships with opium cultivators that vary from symbiotic to despotic. Insecurity reinforces these relationships and this in turn makes the territory easier to penetrate by insurgents.

The feedback loops are evident in southern labor markets. A survey by the Senlis Council, a drug policy advisory forum, suggested that $200–600 per month was offered to work for the Taliban. Law enforcement officials corroborated this in their report stating that the Taliban successfully recruits young locals to fight for $20 a day. These are not hardcore, dedicated and ideological fighters—they are unemployed men, some of whom are accustomed to a mercenary life. Although generally inferior to coalition troops and seemingly deployed in many circumstances as cannon fodder, they can be effective in ambushes and arranging Improvised Explosive Devices (IEDs). Taliban commanders have also used these "tier two" fighters to assist opium harvesting. Harvest time raises the stakes for insurgents in terms of maintaining territorial control. Traditional migrations for seasonal employment supply itinerant laborers who can be employed simultaneously as harvesters and protectors of opium. The Taliban can then take credit for providing local security and ensuring control of opium production.

With the government and coalition unwelcome and subject to active (ambush) and passive (IED) attacks, areas of intense opium cultivation are the most difficult in which to demonstrate any reconstruction and development benefits. Alternative employment for mercenaries and alternative livelihoods for farmer-fighters cannot be delivered and those who might be attracted to such alternatives fear Taliban retribution. For example, the Pajhwok News Agency reported on October 30, 2005 that farmers in the Khan Nishin District in Helmand province were being forced by the Taliban to cultivate poppies under threat of death.

Taxing Opium

Law enforcement officers and UNODC officials interviewed by the authors in April 2007 believe that the "Taliban are completely dependent on the narco-economy for their financing." Where the Taliban are able to enforce it—mostly in the south and some eastern districts—they are said to levy a 40% tax on opium cultivation and trafficking. A low estimate of the amount that the Taliban earn from the opium economy is $10 million, but considering the tradition of imposing tithes on cultivation and activities further up the value chain, the total is likely to be at least $20 million. There are also regular reports of cooperation between political insurgents and profit-driven criminal groups. One example is their collusion to throw small farmers off their land or to indenture them under debts and threats in order to maintain opium production. More detailed information provided to the authors describes arrangements whereby drug traffickers provide money, vehicles and subsistence to Taliban units in return for protection.

The synergy between politically motivated warfare and economic logic is starkly visible and should drive the integration of counter-narcotics and counter-insurgency strategies. Of course, not all violence is linked to transnational jihadis [religious warriors]. Across Afghanistan, profit-driven criminality is more pervasive than sympathy for or cooperation with insurgents, even if both benefit from and contribute to general lawlessness. When it comes to the Taliban, however, the centrality of the opium economy in their funding model is both a strength and a weakness. Reducing their financial power would undermine an important component of their recruitment model. It suggests a potential for turning the vicious circle of insecurity and economic stagnation into a virtuous one of coalition military superiority and job creation.

Counter-Terrorism and Counter-Narcotics

The failure to reduce opium cultivation in the early post-invasion years has directly augmented the Taliban's military strength. They have harvested the opium into weapons. The opiate trade and terrorism activity currently overlap to such an extent that some law enforcement actions fall under counter-narcotics and counter-terrorism simultaneously. So far, despite the millions spent and the various schemes that the coalition has attempted, opium production has increased, maintaining its importance as a source of terrorist funding domestically and internationally. As one Afghan diplomat lamented, "it makes no sense why the donors are blind to what they can see". An integrated approach to counter-terrorism and counter-narcotics is required, taking account of the problem's three major dimensions.

First, proselytizing insurgent groups are treading a fine theological line in financing themselves through drug trafficking. Some drug barons linked with al-Qaeda, such as Badruddoza Chowdhury Momen, have argued that "it is a noble . . . responsibility to spoil Western society with drugs". This line of

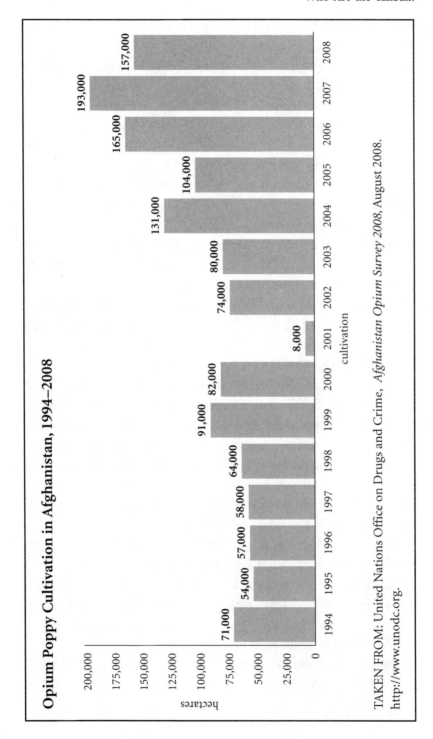

Opium Poppy Cultivation in Afghanistan, 1994–2008

hectares / cultivation

Year	Hectares
1994	71,000
1995	54,000
1996	57,000
1997	58,000
1998	64,000
1999	91,000
2000	82,000
2001	8,000
2002	74,000
2003	80,000
2004	131,000
2005	104,000
2006	165,000
2007	193,000
2008	157,000

TAKEN FROM: United Nations Office on Drugs and Crime, *Afghanistan Opium Survey 2008*, August 2008. http://www.unodc.org.

thought has a long tradition: in 1981, heroin trafficker and mujahideen [Islamic fighter] leader Nasim Akhunzada published a fatwa [Islamic religious edict] stating that "poppy has to be cultivated to finance holy war against Soviet troops and their puppets in Kabul".[1] The difficulty is that most Muslim communities are intolerant of drug use, and to claim that flooding the West with narcotics is a form of jihad glosses over the millions of Muslims addicted to heroin and the associated HIV/AIDS infections. Furthermore, despite the apparently clear religious prohibition on the consumption of intoxicants, the issue appears divisive in the insurgency . . . because some Taliban are drug users themselves.

These contradictions should be exploited in approaches to counter-narcotics operations. Ironically, it was the Taliban who in 2001 produced a successful opium clampdown, justified by religion. The same leaders are now protecting poppy growers from eradication. More than a third of the farmers surveyed by the UNODC who had never planted poppies responded that religion guided their decision. Fear of eradication was a negligible concern. Insurgent justifications depend on potential supporters agreeing that the ends of jihad justify the inherently sinful means. Taliban spokesman Mohammad Hanif summarized the difficult argument for his organization last year [in 2006] when he opposed the cultivation of opium, but was "happy with any means of combating Western societies," including the production of heroin.

Opium eradication is a promising counter-terrorism strategy if it can be executed without damaging the livelihood of the average opium farmer. For every leaflet and exhortation from the insurgents justifying opium, the Afghan government should be there to highlight the Taliban's hypocrisy and advertise the damage done to other Muslims.

Second, development programs that offset farmers' loss of income also need to provide some benefit to the pool of

---

1. The Soviet Union fought Islamic groups for control of Afghanistan in the 1980s.

unemployed workers from which the Taliban recruit. Intervening in the opium economy means re-arranging a number of markets, including those for labor. At least, the under- or unemployed should not be left worse off, although, of course, the better outcome is a self-sustaining development trajectory.

Compensation to farmers is probably necessary. Options for delivering compensation are complicated by the tendency of some farmers to receive loans from traders and insurgents in anticipation of opium delivery, creating a debt burden that requires alleviation. A plan to pay at the end of the planting season is likely to be resisted more strongly. However, payment at the start of the season raises the risks of cheating and also the costs of monitoring since some crops may need to be checked twice. The United Kingdom's payments for not planting in 2002 and 2003 were unsuccessful as farmers (and politicians) pocketed funds and still produced opium. UN [United Nations] officials report that micro-credit programs have often been considered as an alternative to direct subsidies. Essentially, donors would take over the position that money-lenders currently occupy, with lower interest rates and a prohibition on using funds for opium cultivation.

Whatever the offsetting option chosen, the amount pumped into rural economies would need to equal that generated by opium production minus the value of producing licit crops and adhering to socio-religious rules. An eradication program supported by compensation and religious justification would trap the legitimacy of insurgents in a pincer maneuver. President [Hamid] Karzai's 2004 suggestion for a "jihad on drugs" showed the right intent, but the argument needs to be heard at the micro-level through anti-drug proselytizing by local religious leaders. With the precedent of the Taliban's 2001 ban on opium cultivation and a strong effort by the Afghan government—with the help of foreign funds—to buffer the loss of income, incitements to rebellion will be weakened.

Eradicating Drugs Is Key to Success

Finally, the geographical concentration of the insurgency indicates that counter-narcotics tactics need to vary with location. For example, eradication is difficult and possibly counterproductive in Helmand and Kandahar. Less than 10% of Helmand's poppy cultivation was eradicated in 2006, a figure subject to question in light of frequent reports that bribes are successful in avoiding eradication, particularly where government control is weak. Where security is already poor, teams of eradicators are likely to increase support for local insurgents, who by responding violently can demonstrate that they are protecting communities' interests. During counter-insurgency campaigns, policies of attraction are at least as important as those of attrition. This holds true for an integrated counter-narcotics component. In the north and west, there are relatively good prospects for reducing and holding down opium production through a comprehensive approach. Where Kabul and the coalition can exert a degree of effective governance, they can gain trust and promote credible programs. An additional angle that could be considered is a safe biological agent to eradicate and suppress poppy cultivation.

As of November 2006, Afghanistan's Counter-Narcotics Trust Fund had approved only two projects across the south. Where territorial control is hotly disputed or in the hands of the Taliban, the best counter-narcotics policy is benign neglect toward cultivators and attempting to interdict traffickers. Priority districts for implementing comprehensive programs should be those that have a relatively strong coalition/government presence and adjoin to insecure or Taliban-controlled opium-producing areas. Where successful, these demonstrate to others nearby the intent and benefit of government efforts. Perhaps the best way to spread this news is to take participants from one district into adjacent non-compliant or less secure districts to share their experience.

A three-year commitment that integrates secured eradication and economic offsets is a promising alternative to the medium-term uncertainty of facing off against insurgents without attacking their local sources of funding. The current consensus that a decades-long project is required to turn farmers away from opium needs to be challenged by a strategy that views continuing production as a paramount security problem. The economic implications of opium eradication are huge for Afghanistan, but if the country can be secured then the development challenges of the national economy are no greater (or smaller) than those in other destitute states around the world. The difference is that Afghanistan will have removed the primary additional burden it faces: violent terrorist/insurgency activities funded by illicit narcotics.

> "The drug trade is a crucial part of
> Afghanistan's economy. . . . The trade
> is roughly one-third of the country's
> entire gross domestic product."

All of Afghanistan, Not Just the Taliban, Relies on Money from Narcotics

Ted Galen Carpenter

Ted Galen Carpenter is vice president for defense and foreign policy studies at the Cato Institute and author of Bad Neighbor Policy: Washington's Futile War on Drugs in Latin America. *In the following viewpoint, he argues that while poppy cultivation may fund the Taliban, it also is central to economic activity throughout Afghanistan. As a result, he says, an all-out war on drugs in Afghanistan would alienate key allies and much of the population, which depends on money from poppies to survive. Carpenter concludes that the United States should concentrate on fighting al Qaeda and the Taliban and downplay its war on drugs in the region.*

Ted Galen Carpenter, "Afghanistan's Drug Problem," *National Interest*, December 5, 2008. Copyright © 2008 The National Interest, Washington, D.C. Reproduced by permission.

As you read, consider the following questions:

1. According to Carpenter, why are drug trafficking and terrorism connected?
2. Carpenter believes that what percentage of the population of Afghanistan is involved directly or indirectly in the drug trade?
3. What examples does Carpenter give of past situations in which the United States ignored drug trafficking to focus on other priorities?

General James Jones, President-elect [Barack] Obama's choice as national-security adviser, said earlier this week [December 2008] that a more "comprehensive" strategy was needed to defeat the Taliban and al-Qaeda [a terrorist organization] in Afghanistan. Part of his comprehensive approach would be to intensify the campaign against the illegal drug trade. That would be a disastrous mistake. The opium trade is such a huge part of Afghanistan's economy, that efforts to eradicate it would alienate millions of Afghans and play into the hands of the terrorists.

The War on Drugs Is Counterproductive

Under pressure from Washington, [Afghan] President Hamid Karzai has already called on the Afghan people to wage war against narcotics with the same determination and ferocity that they resisted the Soviet occupation in the 1980s. Given the economic and social realities in Afghanistan, that is an unrealistic and potentially very dangerous objective.

Despite the comments of General Jones, there has long been skepticism in U.S. and NATO [North Atlantic Treaty Organization] military circles about the wisdom of pursuing a vigorous war on drugs in Afghanistan. Commanders correctly believe that such an effort complicates their primary mission: eradicating al-Qaeda and Taliban forces.

There is little doubt that al-Qaeda and other anti-government elements profit from the drug trade. What drug warriors refuse to acknowledge is that the connection between drug trafficking and terrorism is a direct result of making drugs illegal, thereby creating an enormous black-market premium. Not surprisingly, terrorist groups in Afghanistan and other countries are quick to exploit such a vast source of potential funding. Absent a worldwide prohibitionist policy, the profit margins in drug trafficking would be a tiny fraction of their current levels, and terrorist groups would have to seek other sources of revenue.

In any case, the United States faces a dilemma if it conducts a vigorous drug-eradication campaign in Afghanistan in an effort to dry up the funds flowing to al-Qaeda and the Taliban. Those are not the only factions involved in drug trafficking. Evidence has emerged that officials in Karzai's government perhaps even the president's brother, are also recipients of largesse from the narcotics trade. Even more important, many of Karzai's political allies are warlords who control the drug commerce in their respective regions. They use the resulting revenues to pay the militias that keep them in power in their fiefdoms and give them national political clout. Some of these individuals backed the Taliban when that faction was in power, switching sides only when the United States launched its military offensive in Afghanistan in October 2001. Antidrug campaigns might cause them to change their allegiance yet again.

In addition to the need to placate cooperative warlords, the U.S.-led coalition relies on poppy growers as spies for information on movements of Taliban and al-Qaeda units. Disrupting the opium crop alienates those vital sources of information.

Drugs and the Economy

The drug trade is a crucial part of Afghanistan's economy. Afghanistan accounts for more than 90 percent of the world's

Afghan Farmers and Poppy Eradication

Doug Wankel [an official in charge of poppy eradication efforts in Afghanistan] walked up to an angry-looking farmer who was watching his field being destroyed and asked him, through an interpreter named Nazeem, how much he got for his opium. Twenty-one thousand Pakistani rupees for a four-kilo package, the farmer said, and he harvested three to four kilos per jirib (a local land measurement equivalent to about half an acre). He added, "I get only a thousand rupees per jirib of wheat, so I'm obliged to grow poppies." That comes to about thirty-three dollars from an acre of wheat, and between five hundred and seven hundred dollars from an acre of poppies. In Uruzgan [an Afghan province], the opium was sold to middlemen who then smuggled it out of Afghanistan to Pakistan or Iran.

"How long have you been growing poppies?" Wankel asked him.

The farmer looked surprised. "When I was born, I saw the poppies," he said.

When we were ready to move on, the farmer said, as if to be polite, "Thank you—but I can't really thank you, because you haven't destroyed just my poppies but my wheat, too." He pointed to where A.T.V.s [all-terrain vehicles] had driven through a wheat patch. Wankel apologized, then commented that it was only one small section. "But you have also damaged my watermelons," the farmer insisted, pointing to another part of the field. "Now I will have nothing left."

Jon Lee Anderson, "The Taliban's Opium War,"
New Yorker, July 9, 2007. www.newyorker.com.

opium supply, and opium poppies are now grown in most provinces. The trade is roughly one-third of the country's entire gross domestic product. According to the United Nations, some five hundred nine thousand Afghan families are involved in opium poppy cultivation. Even measured on a nuclear-family basis, that translates into about 14 percent of Afghanistan's population. Given the role of extended families and clans in Afghan society, the number of people affected is much greater than that. Indeed, it is likely that at least 35 percent of the population is involved directly or indirectly in the drug trade. For many of those people, opium poppy crops and other aspects of drug commerce are the difference between modest prosperity (by Afghan standards) and destitution. They do not look kindly on efforts to destroy their livelihood.

Despite those daunting economic factors, the [George W.] Bush administration has put increased pressure on the Karzai government to crack down on the drug trade, and the incoming Obama administration apparently intends to continue that strategy. The Afghan regime is responding cautiously, trying to convince Washington that it is serious about dealing with the problem without launching a full-blown antidrug crusade that will alienate large segments of the population. It has tried to achieve that balance by focusing on high-profile raids against drug-processing labs—mostly those that are not controlled by warlords friendly to the Kabul government. Afghan officials have been especially adamant in opposing the aerial spraying of poppy fields—a strategy that Washington has successfully pushed allied governments in Colombia and other South American drug-source countries to do.

Washington's pressure on Karzai is myopic. The Taliban and their al-Qaeda allies are rapidly regaining strength, especially in Helmand and Kandahar provinces, perhaps not coincidentally the areas of the most vigorous antidrug campaigns.

If zealous American drug warriors alienate hundreds of thousands of Afghan farmers, the Karzai government's hold on power could become even more precarious. Washington would then face the unpalatable choice of risking the reemergence of chaos in Afghanistan, including the prospect that radical Islamists might regain power, or sending more U.S. troops to stabilize the situation beyond the reinforcements already contemplated for 2009.

The Drug War Should Not Be a Priority

U.S. officials need to keep their priorities straight. Our mortal enemy is al-Qaeda and the Taliban regime that made Afghanistan into a sanctuary for that terrorist organization. The drug war is a dangerous distraction in the campaign to destroy those forces. Recognizing that security considerations sometimes trump other objectives would hardly be an unprecedented move by Washington. U.S. agencies quietly ignored drug-trafficking activities of anticommunist factions in Central America during the 1980s when the primary goal was to keep those countries out of the Soviet orbit. In the early 1990s, the United States also eased its pressure on Peru's government regarding the drug-eradication issue when President Alberto Fujimori concluded that a higher priority had to be given to winning coca farmers away from the Maoist Shining Path guerrilla movement.

The Obama administration should adopt a similar pragmatic policy in Afghanistan and look the other way regarding the drug-trafficking activities of friendly warlords. And above all, the U.S. military must not become the enemy of Afghan farmers whose livelihood depends on opium-poppy cultivation. True, some of the funds from the drug trade will find their way into the coffers of the Taliban and al-Qaeda. That is an inevitable side effect of a global prohibitionist policy that creates such an enormous profit from illegal drugs. But alienating pro-Western Afghan factions in an effort to disrupt the flow of revenue to the Islamic radicals is too high a price to pay. General Jones should reconsider his views.

Periodical Bibliography

The following articles have been selected to supplement the diverse views presented in this chapter.

Peter Bergen   "The Taliban-Al Qaeda Merger," *The New Republic*, October 19, 2009.

Giles Dorronsoro   "Who Are the Taliban?" *Carnegie Endowment for International Peace*, October 22, 2009.

Barbara Ellis   "Know Thine Enemy," *Foreign Affairs*, November 2, 2009.

Ellen Goodman   "Afghanistan's Forgotten Class," *Boston Globe*, November 6, 2009.

Anand Gopal   "What You Should Know About Women's Rights in Afghanistan," *Huffington Post*, April 13, 2009.

Irfan Husain   "What the Taliban Want," Dawn.com, January 23, 2010.

Julien Mercille   "U.N. Report Misleading on Afghanistan's Drug Problem," *Foreign Policy in Focus*, November 5, 2009.

Joshua Partlow   "In Afghanistan, Taliban Surpasses al-Qaeda," *Washington Post*, November 11, 2009.

David Rohde   "Terrorists Without Borders," *The New Republic*, February 23, 2010.

Reihan Salam   "The Taliban-Al Qaeda Connection," *The Daily Beast*, October 16, 2009.

OPPOSING
VIEWPOINTS®
SERIES

CHAPTER 2

How Should the United States Deal with the Taliban?

Chapter Preface

In 2001, the Taliban were in control of Afghanistan. Their regime was brutally and notoriously repressive, especially to women. Furthermore, they were known to be harboring Osama bin Laden, who was responsible for the September 11, 2001, terrorist attacks that killed thousands in the United States. The U.S. decision to pursue bin Laden by invading Afghanistan in late 2001 was, therefore, "widely popular in both the United States and Europe," according to Robert Farley in an October 27, 2006, article in *American Prospect*. As President Barack Obama pointed out in a speech at West Point on December 1, 2009, "The vote in the Senate [authorizing the attack on Afghanistan in 2001] was 98 to nothing. The vote in the House was 420 to 1. For the first time in its history, the North Atlantic Treaty Organization (NATO) invoked Article 5—the commitment that says an attack on one member nation is an attack on all. And the United Nations Security Council endorsed the use of all necessary steps to respond to the 9/11 attacks."

As the war in Afghanistan dragged on, however, and the insurgency showed little sign of abating, public support for the war among Americans gradually declined. According to polls listed in a June 26, 2006, *USA Today* article, 89 percent of respondents approved of the invasion of Afghanistan in early 2002, shortly after the invasion occurred. By mid-2004, approval had dropped, but remained high at 72 percent.

Five years later, however, support for the war had significantly eroded. In early 2009, a majority of respondents, 52 percent, said it believed the war in Afghanistan was a mistake, with only 42 percent saying it was not a mistake, according to Tom Vanden Brook writing in a March 16, 2009, article in *USA Today*. In the same article, the drop in public support was attributed to "seven years of fighting and security trends continuing to point downward."

Still, public opinion has not turned decisively against the Afghan war. A Quinnipiac University poll in April 2010 showed that President Barack Obama's troop increase in Afghanistan was somewhat popular, with 49 percent approving of Obama's handling of the situation and 56 percent agreeing that the United States was doing the "right thing" in fighting the war. Sue Pleming writing on the *Reuters* Web site in an April 22, 2010, article noted that the Quinnipiac University poll "must be welcome" to war supporters since it showed a significant turnaround from negative attitudes toward the war expressed by voters in 2009.

The viewpoints in this chapter present differing views about whether the war in Afghanistan is worth pursuing, and the authors offer various opinions about the ways in which the United States should deal with the Taliban.

> "I am convinced that our security is at stake in Afghanistan and Pakistan. This is the epicenter of violent extremism practiced by al Qaeda."

The Taliban Threaten Vital U.S. Interests

Barack Obama

Barack Obama is the 44th president of the United States. In the following viewpoint he argues that fighting the Taliban in Afghanistan and Pakistan is vital to U.S. interests. The terrorist group al Qaeda has historical links with the Taliban, he argues, and will use Afghanistan and Pakistan as a safe haven if they are not stopped. The presence of the Taliban and al Qaeda in Pakistan is especially dangerous, he contends, because Pakistan has nuclear weapons. Given these concerns, Obama says the United States will increase troop presence in Afghanistan and create a closer partnership with the Pakistani government.

As you read, consider the following questions:

1. What signs of political and international unity does Obama say occurred following the September 11, 2001, terrorist attacks?

Barack Obama, "Remarks by the President in Address to the Nation on the Way Forward in Afghanistan and Pakistan," www.whitehouse.gov, December 1, 2009.

2. When he took office, how many American troops does Obama say were in Iraq and how many were in Afghanistan?

3. According to Obama, when will U.S. forces begin to transfer out of Afghanistan?

It's important to recall why America and our allies were compelled to fight a war in Afghanistan in the first place. We did not ask for this fight. On September 11, 2001, 19 men hijacked four airplanes and used them to murder nearly 3,000 people. They struck at our military and economic nerve centers. They took the lives of innocent men, women, and children without regard to their faith or race or station. Were it not for the heroic actions of passengers onboard one of those flights [who fought the hijackers and forced them to crash the plane], they could have also struck at one of the great symbols of our democracy in Washington [probably either the White House or the capitol building], and killed many more.

Al Qaeda and the Taliban

As we know, these men belonged to al Qaeda—a group of extremists who have distorted and defiled Islam, one of the world's great religions, to justify the slaughter of innocents. Al Qaeda's base of operations was in Afghanistan, where they were harbored by the Taliban—a ruthless, repressive and radical movement that seized control of that country [in the mid-1990s] after it was ravaged by years of Soviet occupation and civil war, and after the attention of America and our friends had turned elsewhere.

Just days after 9/11, Congress authorized the use of force against al Qaeda and those who harbored them—an authorization that continues to this day. The vote in the Senate was 98 to nothing. The vote in the House was 420 to 1. For the first time in its history, the North Atlantic Treaty Organization [NATO] invoked Article 5—the commitment that says an attack on one member nation is an attack on all. And the United Nations [U.N.] Security Council endorsed the use of all necessary steps to respond to the 9/11 attacks. America, our allies and the world were acting as one to destroy al Qaeda's terrorist network and to protect our common security.

Under the banner of this domestic unity and international legitimacy—and only after the Taliban refused to turn over Osama bin Laden [the leader of al Qaeda]—we sent our troops into Afghanistan. Within a matter of months, al Qaeda was scattered and many of its operatives were killed. The Taliban was driven from power and pushed back on its heels. A place that had known decades of fear now had reason to hope. At a conference convened by the U.N., a provisional government was established under President Hamid Karzai. And an International Security Assistance Force [ISAF] was established to help bring a lasting peace to a war-torn country.

War in Iraq

Then, in early 2003, the decision was made to wage a second war, in Iraq. The wrenching debate over the Iraq war is well-known and need not be repeated here. It's enough to say that for the next six years, the Iraq war drew the dominant share of our troops, our resources, our diplomacy, and our national attention—and that the decision to go into Iraq caused substantial rifts between America and much of the world.

Today, after extraordinary costs, we are bringing the Iraq war to a responsible end. We will remove our combat brigades from Iraq by the end of next summer [2010], and all of our troops by the end of 2011. That we are doing so is a testament to the character of the men and women in uniform. Thanks to their courage, grit and perseverance, we have given Iraqis a chance to shape their future, and we are successfully leaving Iraq to its people.

But while we've achieved hard-earned milestones in Iraq, the situation in Afghanistan has deteriorated. After escaping across the border into Pakistan in 2001 and 2002, al Qaeda's leadership established a safe haven there. Although a legitimate government was elected by the Afghan people, it's been hampered by corruption, the drug trade, an under-developed economy, and insufficient security forces.

Over the last several years, the Taliban has maintained common cause with al Qaeda, as they both seek an overthrow of the Afghan government. Gradually, the Taliban has begun to control additional swaths of territory in Afghanistan, while engaging in increasingly brazen and devastating attacks of terrorism against the Pakistani people.

Now, throughout this period, our troop levels in Afghanistan remained a fraction of what they were in Iraq. When I took office, we had just over 32,000 Americans serving in Afghanistan, compared to 160,000 in Iraq at the peak of the war. Commanders in Afghanistan repeatedly asked for support to deal with the reemergence of the Taliban, but these reinforcements did not arrive. And that's why, shortly after taking office [in early 2009], I approved a longstanding request for more troops. After consultations with our allies, I then announced a strategy recognizing the fundamental connection between our war effort in Afghanistan and the extremist safe havens in Pakistan. I set a goal that was narrowly defined as disrupting, dismantling, and defeating al Qaeda and its extremist allies, and pledged to better coordinate our military and civilian efforts.

Progress Has Been Made

Since then, we've made progress on some important objectives. High-ranking al Qaeda and Taliban leaders have been killed, and we've stepped up the pressure on al Qaeda worldwide. In Pakistan, that nation's army has gone on its largest offensive in years. In Afghanistan, we and our allies prevented the Taliban from stopping a presidential election [in 2009], and—although it was marred by fraud—that election produced a government that is consistent with Afghanistan laws and constitution.

Yet huge challenges remain. Afghanistan is not lost, but for several years it has moved backwards. There's no imminent threat of the government being overthrown, but the Taliban has gained momentum. Al Qaeda has not reemerged in Afghanistan in the same numbers as before 9/11, but they retain their safe havens along the border. And our forces lack the full support they need to effectively train and partner with Afghan security forces and better secure the population. Our new commander in Afghanistan—General [Stanley] McChrystal—has reported that the security situation is more serious than he anticipated. In short: The status quo is not sustainable. . . .

After the Afghan voting was completed, I insisted on a thorough review of our strategy. Now, let me be clear: There has never been an option before me that called for troop deployments before 2010, so there has been no delay or denial of resources necessary for the conduct of the war during this review period. Instead, the review has allowed me to ask the hard questions, and to explore all the different options along with my national security team, our military and civilian leadership in Afghanistan, and our key partners. And given the stakes involved, I owed the American people—and our troops—no less.

This review is now complete. And as Commander-in-Chief, I have determined that it is in our vital national interest to send an additional 30,000 U.S. troops to Afghanistan. After 18 months, our troops will begin to come home. These are the resources that we need to seize the initiative, while building the Afghan capacity that can allow for a responsible transition of our forces out of Afghanistan.

American Security Is at Stake in Afghanistan

I do not make this decision lightly. I opposed the war in Iraq precisely because I believe that we must exercise restraint in the use of military force, and always consider the long-term consequences of our actions. We have been at war now for eight years, at enormous cost in lives and resources. Years of debate over Iraq and terrorism have left our unity on national security issues in tatters, and created a highly polarized and partisan backdrop for this effort. And having just experienced the worst economic crisis since the Great Depression [the financial crisis of 2007–2009], the American people are understandably focused on rebuilding our economy and putting people to work here at home.

Most of all, I know that this decision asks even more of . . . a military that . . . , has already borne the heaviest of all burdens. As President, I have signed a letter of condolence to the family of each American who gives their life in these wars. I have read the letters from the parents and spouses of those deployed. I visited our courageous wounded warriors at Walter Reed [Army Medical Center]. I've traveled to Dover [Del.] to meet the flag-draped caskets of 18 Americans returning home to their final resting place. I see firsthand the terrible wages of war. If I did not think that the security of the United States and the safety of the American people were at stake in Afghanistan, I would gladly order every single one of our troops home tomorrow.

So, no, I do not make this decision lightly. I make this decision because I am convinced that our security is at stake in Afghanistan and Pakistan. This is the epicenter of violent extremism practiced by al Qaeda. It is from here that we were attacked on 9/11, and it is from here that new attacks are being plotted as I speak. This is no idle danger; no hypothetical threat. In the last few months alone, we have apprehended extremists within our borders who were sent here from the border region of Afghanistan and Pakistan to commit new acts of terror. And this danger will only grow if the region slides backwards, and al Qaeda can operate with impunity. We must keep the pressure on al Qaeda, and to do that, we must increase the stability and capacity of our partners in the region.

Of course, this burden is not ours alone to bear. This is not just America's war. Since 9/11, al Qaeda's safe havens have been the source of attacks against London and Amman and Bali.[1] The people and governments of both Afghanistan and Pakistan are endangered. And the stakes are even higher within a nuclear-armed Pakistan, because we know that al Qaeda and other extremists seek nuclear weapons, and we have every reason to believe that they would use them.

Disrupt, Dismantle, and Defeat al Qaeda

These facts compel us to act along with our friends and allies. Our overarching goal remains the same: to disrupt, dismantle, and defeat al Qaeda in Afghanistan and Pakistan, and to prevent its capacity to threaten America and our allies in the future.

To meet that goal, we will pursue the following objectives within Afghanistan. We must deny al Qaeda a safe haven. We must reverse the Taliban's momentum and deny it the ability to overthrow the government. And we must strengthen the capacity of Afghanistan's security forces and government so that they can take lead responsibility for Afghanistan's future.

We will meet these objectives in three ways. First, we will pursue a military strategy that will break the Taliban's momentum and increase Afghanistan's capacity over the next 18 months.

The 30,000 additional troops that I'm announcing tonight will deploy in the first part of 2010—the fastest possible pace—so that they can target the insurgency and secure key

1. Al Qaeda is thought to be responsible for bombings in Bali, Indonesia, in 2002; bombings in Amman, Jordan, in 2005; and bombings in London in 2005.

The Surge Will Work

As the Afghan surge [in troop levels] gets under way in 2009, the pundits are as pessimistic as they were about Iraq in 2007 [when troop levels were increased]. But the surge will work, because Gen. Stanley McChrystal, the top commander in Afghanistan, has shown every indication that he's learned the lessons of the Iraqi experience. He's already pushed for a serious investigation into a NATO [North Atlantic Treaty Organization] bomb attack in September [2009] that killed several civilians. McChrystal, in other words, is serious about protecting the population. That will help the U.S. military receive more and better intelligence as they spread out into communities and signal their commitment to ensuring safety. The secrets of the Taliban's logistical networks and hideouts will be revealed, paving the way for a crushing offense.

Newsweek, *"#1 The Afghan Surge Works—World Predictions—Newsweek 2010,"* www.newsweek.com.

population centers. They'll increase our ability to train competent Afghan security forces, and to partner with them so that more Afghans can get into the fight. And they will help create the conditions for the United States to transfer responsibility to the Afghans.

Because this is an international effort, I've asked that our commitment be joined by contributions from our allies. Some have already provided additional troops, and we're confident that there will be further contributions in the days and weeks ahead. Our friends have fought and bled and died alongside us in Afghanistan. And now, we must come together to end this war successfully. For what's at stake is not simply a test of

NATO's credibility—what's at stake is the security of our allies, and the common security of the world.

But taken together, these additional American and international troops will allow us to accelerate handing over responsibility to Afghan forces, and allow us to begin the transfer of our forces out of Afghanistan in July of 2011. Just as we have done in Iraq, we will execute this transition responsibly, taking into account conditions on the ground. We'll continue to advise and assist Afghanistan's security forces to ensure that they can succeed over the long haul. But it will be clear to the Afghan government—and, more importantly, to the Afghan people—that they will ultimately be responsible for their own country.

Second, we will work with our partners, the United Nations, and the Afghan people to pursue a more effective civilian strategy, so that the government can take advantage of improved security.

This effort must be based on performance. The days of providing a blank check are over. President Karzai's inauguration speech sent the right message about moving in a new direction. And going forward, we will be clear about what we expect from those who receive our assistance. We'll support Afghan ministries, governors, and local leaders that combat corruption and deliver for the people. We expect those who are ineffective or corrupt to be held accountable. And we will also focus our assistance in areas—such as agriculture—that can make an immediate impact in the lives of the Afghan people.

The people of Afghanistan have endured violence for decades. They've been confronted with occupation—by the Soviet Union [in the 1980s], and then by foreign al Qaeda fighters who used Afghan land for their own purposes. So tonight, I want the Afghan people to understand—America seeks an end to this era of war and suffering. We have no interest in occupying your country. We will support efforts by the Afghan government to open the door to those Taliban who abandon violence and respect the human rights of their fellow citizens. And we will seek a partnership with Afghanistan grounded in mutual respect—to isolate those who destroy; to strengthen those who build; to hasten the day when our troops will leave; and to forge a lasting friendship in which America is your partner, and never your patron.

A Partnership with Pakistan

Third, we will act with the full recognition that our success in Afghanistan is inextricably linked to our partnership with Pakistan.

We're in Afghanistan to prevent a cancer from once again spreading through that country. But this same cancer has also taken root in the border region of Pakistan. That's why we need a strategy that works on both sides of the border.

In the past, there have been those in Pakistan who've argued that the struggle against extremism is not their fight, and that Pakistan is better off doing little or seeking accommodation with those who use violence. But in recent years, as innocents have been killed from Karachi to Islamabad, it has become clear that it is the Pakistani people who are the most endangered by extremism. Public opinion has turned. The Pakistani army has waged an offensive in Swat and South Waziristan [parts of northwest Pakistan near the Afghani border]. And there is no doubt that the United States and Pakistan share a common enemy.

In the past, we too often defined our relationship with Pakistan narrowly. Those days are over. Moving forward, we are committed to a partnership with Pakistan that is built on a foundation of mutual interest, mutual respect, and mutual trust. We will strengthen Pakistan's capacity to target those groups that threaten our countries, and have made it clear that we cannot tolerate a safe haven for terrorists whose location is known and whose intentions are clear. America is also providing substantial resources to support Pakistan's democracy and development. We are the largest international supporter for those Pakistanis displaced by the fighting. And going forward, the Pakistan people must know America will remain a strong supporter of Pakistan's security and prosperity long after the guns have fallen silent, so that the great potential of its people can be unleashed.

These are the three core elements of our strategy: a military effort to create the conditions for a transition; a civilian surge that reinforces positive action; and an effective partnership with Pakistan.

"We must see jihadists for the small, lethal, disjointed and miserable opponents that they are."

The Taliban Are Not a Threat
to the United States

John Mueller

*John Mueller is professor of political science at Ohio State Uni-
versity and author of* Overblown: How Politicians and the Terrorism Industry Inflate National Security Threats, and Why
We Believe Them. *In the following viewpoint, he argues that the
Taliban are unlikely to provide a useful safe haven for al Qaeda
if they gain control of Afghanistan. Moreover, he says, al Qaeda
itself is small, weak, and increasingly unpopular in the Muslim
world. Mueller concludes that the Taliban are not a real security
threat, and suggests that as a result the Afghan war is likely to
become increasingly unpopular in the United States.*

As you read, consider the following questions:

1. What does Mueller say that conspiracies involving small
   numbers of people require, and what does he say they
   do not require?

2. Outside of war zones, how many deaths are perpetrated each year by al Qaeda affiliates, according to Mueller?

3. According to Mueller, what is the problem with basing the war in Afghanistan on humanitarian motives?

George W. Bush led the United States into war in Iraq on the grounds that [Iraqi President] Saddam Hussein might give his country's nonexistent weapons of mass destruction to terrorists. Now, Bush's successor [President Barack Obama] is perpetuating the war in Afghanistan with comparably dubious arguments about the danger posed by the Taliban and [terrorist group] al Qaeda.

The Taliban Will Not Host al Qaeda

President Barack Obama insists that the U.S. mission in Afghanistan is about "making sure that al Qaeda cannot attack the U.S. homeland and U.S. interests and our allies" or "project violence against" American citizens. The reasoning is that if the Taliban win in Afghanistan, al Qaeda will once again be able to set up shop there to carry out its dirty work. As the president puts it, Afghanistan would "again be a base for terrorists who want to kill as many of our people as they possibly can." This argument is constantly repeated but rarely examined; given the costs and risks associated with the Obama administration's plans for the region, it is time such statements be given the scrutiny they deserve.

Multiple sources, including Lawrence Wright's book *The Looming Tower*, make clear that the Taliban was a reluctant host to al Qaeda in the 1990s and felt betrayed when the terrorist group repeatedly violated agreements to refrain from issuing inflammatory statements and fomenting violence abroad. Then the al Qaeda-sponsored 9/11 attacks [the September 11, 2001, attacks on the United States]—which the Taliban had nothing to do with—led to the toppling of the

Al Qaida Is Weakened

JIM LEHRER [reporter]: Should al-Qaida still be seen as a threat to the homeland of the United States of America, Mr. Carle?

GLENN CARLE [former Central Intelligence Agency (CIA) official]: The one-word answer is yes.... It will be a threat so long as there's one individual who's coherent enough to plan and try to execute an operation.

But, as an institution, as an entity, it is substantially weaker than it was, and it was never as dramatically strong as our fears would have imagined.

Jim Lehrer, "Al-Qaida 'on the Run,' CIA Chief Panetta Says,"
PBS News Hour, March 18, 2010. www.pbs.org.

Taliban's regime. Given the Taliban's limited interest in issues outside the "AfPak" [Afghanistan-Pakistan] region, if they came to power again now, they would be highly unlikely to host provocative terrorist groups whose actions could lead to another outside intervention. And even if al Qaeda were able to relocate to Afghanistan after a Taliban victory there, it would still have to operate under the same siege situation it presently enjoys in what Obama calls its "safe haven" in Pakistan.

The very notion that al Qaeda needs a secure geographic base to carry out its terrorist operations, moreover, is questionable. After all, the operational base for 9/11 was in Hamburg, Germany. Conspiracies involving small numbers of people require communication, money, and planning—but not a major protected base camp.

The Safety of the World Is Not at Stake

At present, al Qaeda consists of a few hundred people running around in Pakistan, seeking to avoid detection and helping the Taliban when possible. It also has a disjointed network of fellow travelers around the globe who communicate over the Internet. Over the last decade, the group has almost completely discredited itself in the Muslim world due to the fallout from the 9/11 attacks and subsequent counterproductive terrorism, much of it directed against Muslims. No convincing evidence has been offered publicly to show that al Qaeda Central has put together a single full operation anywhere in the world since 9/11. And, outside of war zones, the violence perpetrated by al Qaeda affiliates, wannabes, and lookalikes combined has resulted in the deaths of some 200 to 300 people per year, and may be declining. That is 200 to 300 too many, of course, but it scarcely suggests that "the safety of people around the world is at stake," as Obama dramatically puts it.

In addition, al Qaeda has yet to establish a significant presence in the United States. In 2002, U.S. intelligence reports asserted that the number of trained al Qaeda operatives in the United States was between 2,000 and 5,000, and FBI [Federal Bureau of Investigation] Director Robert Mueller assured a Senate committee that al Qaeda had "developed a support infrastructure" in the country and achieved both "the ability and the intent to inflict significant casualties in the U.S. with little warning." However, after years of well funded sleuthing, the FBI and other investigative agencies have been unable to uncover a single true al Qaeda sleeper cell or operative within the country. Mueller's rallying cry has now been reduced to a comparatively bland formulation: "We believe al Qaeda is still seeking to infiltrate operatives into the U.S. from overseas."

Even that may not be true. Since 9/11, some two million foreigners have been admitted to the United States legally and many others, of course, have entered illegally. Even if border security has been so effective that 90 percent of al Qaeda's operatives have been turned away or deterred from entering the United States, some should have made it in—and some of those, it seems reasonable to suggest, would have been picked up by law enforcement by now. The lack of attacks inside the United States combined with the inability of the FBI to find any potential attackers suggests that the terrorists are either not trying very hard or are far less clever and capable than usually depicted.

Miserable Opponents

Policymakers and the public at large should keep in mind the words of Glenn Carle, a 23 year veteran of the CIA [Central Intelligence Agency] who served as deputy national intelligence officer for transnational threats: "We must see jihadists for the small, lethal, disjointed and miserable opponents that they are." Al Qaeda "has only a handful of individuals capable of planning, organizing and leading a terrorist operation," Carle notes, and "its capabilities are far inferior to its desires."

President Obama has said that there is also a humanitarian element to the Afghanistan mission. A return of the Taliban, he points out, would condemn the Afghan people "to brutal governance, international isolation, a paralyzed economy, and the denial of basic human rights." This concern is legitimate—the Afghan people appear to be quite strongly opposed to a return of the Taliban, and they are surely entitled to some peace after 30 years of almost continual warfare, much of it imposed on them from outside.

The problem, as Obama is doubtlessly well aware, is that Americans are far less willing to sacrifice lives for missions that are essentially humanitarian than for those that seek to deal with a threat directed at the United States itself. People who embrace the idea of a humanitarian mission will continue to support Obama's policy in Afghanistan—at least if they think it has a chance of success—but many Americans (and Europeans) will increasingly start to question how many lives such a mission is worth.

This questioning, in fact, is well under way. Because of its ties to 9/11, the war in Afghanistan has enjoyed considerably greater public support than the war in Iraq did (or, for that matter, the wars in Korea or Vietnam). However, there has been a considerable dropoff in that support of late. If Obama's national security justification for his war in Afghanistan comes to seem as spurious as Bush's national security justification for his war in Iraq, he, like Bush, will increasingly have only the humanitarian argument to fall back on. And that is likely to be a weak reed.

> *"I personally think that the military operations themselves are failing because there has been no coherent theaterwide counterinsurgency strategy in Afghanistan."*

The Taliban Are Winning the War in Afghanistan

Kimberly Kagan

Kimberly Kagan is president of the Institute for the Study of War and the author of The Surge: A Military History. *In the following viewpoint, she argues that the United States is losing the war in Afghanistan because it has not concentrated forces in the right places, because it does not take enough time to secure important areas, because it focuses too much on development and too little on security, and because it has not done a good job of measuring success or failure. Kagan says that victory in Afghanistan is possible, but it will require a prompt change in strategy.*

As you read, consider the following questions:

1. Kagan believes the United States should put more troops in what area?

Kimberly Kagan, "Why the Taliban Are Winning—For Now," *Foreign Policy*, August 10, 2009. Copyright © 2009 by the Council on Foreign Relations, Inc. Reproduced by permission of the publisher. www.foreignaffairs.org.

2. What is the ring road, according to the viewpoint?

3. Why does Kagan believe that it is good news that the United States has not been doing the right things for the past few years in Afghanistan?

The war in Afghanistan has not been going well, and it is no surprise that Americans are frustrated. Many observers can rightly point to signs of progress: the functionality of specific Afghan government ministries and programs, the slow growth of the Afghan National Army, the building of major infrastructure such as roads and dams, and agricultural improvements. These accomplishments, however, have not created the conditions that the United States has aimed to achieve: an Afghan state with a competent government considered legitimate by its people and capable of defending them, such that Afghanistan can no longer function as a safe haven for Islamist terrorist groups. Indeed, as Gen. Stanley McChrystal, commander of coalition forces, recently suggested, the situation shows signs of deteriorating: Afghan enemy groups remain highly capable, have gained momentum, and have expanded their areas of operations. Violence against coalition forces is rising. So the question is: Why haven't we been winning in Afghanistan?

Although I served on McChrystal's assessment team, I do not know how he would answer this question, nor could I speculate about his recommendations for the strategy going forward. But after much research, as well as two visits to Afghanistan this year, I personally think that the military operations themselves are failing because there has been no coherent theaterwide counterinsurgency strategy in Afghanistan. Despite U.S. President Barack Obama's newly announced [as of early 2009] "Af-Pak" [Afghanistan-Pakistan] strategy, the U.S. and coalition campaign this summer is a continuation of the poorly designed operations from 2008. And the sheer inertia of military operations means that it will be hard to turn this supertanker around for the better part of this year. But turn it around we must, starting with correcting the following flaws in the strategy that McChrystal and his team inherited from their predecessors.

Fighting in the Wrong Places

NATO [North Atlantic Treaty Organization] forces are widely dispersed throughout Afghanistan, even in the Pashtun areas in the south and east [that is, in areas dominated by ethnic Pashtuns, where the Taliban is strongest], rather than concentrated on one or two priorities. A possible exception is Helmand, the only province in which two brigades are deployed— the British force and the recently arrived U.S. Marine expeditionary brigade. In contrast, during the surge in Iraq [in 2007, when the U.S. increased troop levels], the United States concentrated about half of its forces in Baghdad [the capital of Iraq] and its suburbs. Baghdad was the center of gravity of the fight. If we controlled it, we'd win; if the enemy controlled it, we'd lose. So five brigade combat teams—roughly 25,000 troops with their enablers—protected the city of 8 million people. Four more teams protected Baghdad's southern approaches, and at least one, sometimes two, additional teams protected the city's northern suburbs.

There is no simple equivalent to Baghdad in Afghanistan. Instead, most of the population—and the insurgency—is dispersed in rural areas. Nevertheless, some areas, such as Kandahar city and the districts around it, are more important—to the enemy, to the Afghan government, and to us—than others. And yet, there are almost no counterinsurgents whatsoever in all but two of the districts around Kandahar, and none in the city itself, just a scant footprint from the Afghanistan national security forces. Worse still, the ratio of counterinsurgents to the population in those two districts is approximately 1 to 44, close to the minimum requirement. A good evaluation of our priorities in Afghanistan would yield a significantly different, and more effective, distribution of coalition forces. This is undoubtedly why McChrystal recently told reporters that he will be concentrating forces around Kandahar city.

Fighting in the Wrong Ways

Another problem is that NATO forces have briefed counterinsurgency doctrine better than they have practiced it. Almost all NATO units in Pashtun areas claim that they are protecting the population by engaging in a sequence of military operations known as "shape-clear-hold-build." But these forces move through the sequence too rapidly. Based on recent experiences in Iraq, shaping an area requires 30 to 45 days, clearing it requires three to six months, and holding it takes longer than that. With very few exceptions, NATO forces in Afghanistan have never operated on such timelines. They condense shaping and clearing operations into a few weeks, and then they transition prematurely into what they perceive as a hold phase. As a result, NATO forces rarely gain permanent control over areas—or if they do, those areas are so small as to have little effect on the insurgency or the population. The enemy simply dissipates and then returns.

What's more, coalition and Afghan forces are excessively focused on securing supply lines and reducing the threat of improvised explosive devices through tactical efforts rather than by countering the insurgency. Consequently, many forces—especially Afghan forces—are distributed along the ring road, the main corridor that circles the country. Static positions such as these waste troops. Of course, our forces must be able to maneuver along strategic corridors, but the best way to do that is by securing populated areas and maneuvering off the ring road to defeat the enemy in its sanctuaries and support zones.

In other areas, combat forces are trying to do the right things but, again, in the wrong places. As the Iraq experience demonstrated, successful counterinsurgency often entails dis-

The Taliban Are Winning the Propaganda War

The Taliban has created a sophisticated communications apparatus that projects an increasingly confident movement. Using the full range of media, it is successfully tapping into strains of Afghan nationalism and exploiting policy failures by the Kabul [capital city] government and its international backers. The result is weakening public support for nation-building, even though few actively support the Taliban.

"Taliban Propaganda: Winning the War of Words,"
International Crisis Group, July 24, 2008. www.crisisgroup.org.

tributing forces from larger to smaller bases in order to live among the population. But in some remote areas of Afghanistan's eastern theater, such as Nuristan, where the enemy has little operational or strategic effect, combat forces have overextended themselves. They have moved off large forward operating bases, pushed into strategically insignificant areas, and established small combat outposts that can barely sustain themselves: The units there are too tiny to do anything but protect their outpost. A better approach is to concentrate forces for counterinsurgency operations and run greater risks in places of lesser importance.

Fighting with the Wrong Assumptions

What too often determines where coalition forces conduct their shape-clear-hold-build operations is the prospect for conducting development projects—not population security. This tends to favor the important over the urgent, the possible over the necessary. For example, major combat operations in the British area of Helmand have been conducted in order to permit development. The Kajaki dam and the agricultural development zone near Lashkar Gah have driven the concentration of forces within the province and, indeed, within the southern region generally. In eastern Afghanistan, U.S. forces have conducted operations to build roads, such as the Khost-Gardez Pass road. These projects are important for long-term development, but they are only sometimes important for achieving our military objectives and should not be allowed to dictate the disposition of scarce military resources.

Moreover, military and civilian efforts in Afghanistan make the wrong assumptions about development. Too often they emphasize the value of a development project as a model—as a demonstration of Afghan government competence and Western goodwill. Completing a specific dam, for example, shows the population that the Afghan government can provide services in general; clearing a specific village shows that the Afghan national security forces can secure the population in principle. But if the model is not replicated widely and rapidly, it's simply a demonstration of what might be accomplished. Demonstration effects will not defeat the insurgency. Either a venue is secure and has an operating government, or it does not. A good counterinsurgency plan succeeds by generating synergies among good, localized projects—not by identifying a thousand points of light and hoping that they constitute an electrical grid.

Fighting Successfully—or Failing?

Metrics are important in any war, and based on recent reports, the Obama administration is preparing a new set of indicators to measure whether the fight in Afghanistan is succeeding. As important as identifying good metrics is rejecting bad ones. Violence against coalition forces, for example, is an unreliable indicator of success or failure. For one thing, as we saw in Iraq, violence against friendly forces can increase at the start of a counteroffensive to regain control of areas that the enemy holds. No violence, in turn, might mean that an area is completely controlled by the enemy. The metrics of success are not simply statistics, and they cannot be determined independently of a campaign plan, which sets out a hierarchy of tasks and objectives.

Can We Win?

Some answer simply and sharply in the negative: They claim that Afghanistan has never been centrally ruled (which is wrong) and that it has been the "graveyard of empires" (which is true in only a specific handful of cases). Failure is not at all inevitable. The war in Afghanistan has suffered almost from the start from a lack of resources, especially the time and attention of senior policymakers. The United States prioritized the war in Iraq from 2007 until 2009, for strategically sound reasons. Some of this parsimony also comes from flawed theories of counterinsurgency: U.S. Secretary of Defense Robert Gates, for example, misreads the Soviet experience in Afghanistan [in the 1980s, when the Soviets fought to control and lost Afghanistan], which has consistently led him to argue incorrectly against expanding the size of the force there, claiming that it increases the risks of failure.

We can win in Afghanistan, but only if we restructure the campaign and resource it properly. Adding more resources to the military effort as it has been conducted over the past few years, without fundamentally changing its conception, design, and execution, would achieve little. This was also the case in Iraq before the surge, and the change in strategy and campaign plan that followed was as important to success as the additional resources. This explains why McChrystal might adopt a different campaign design—perhaps requiring additional military resources—when he submits his formal assessment to the U.S. secretary of defense and NATO secretary-general sometime after the Afghan elections.

The fact that we have not been doing the right things for the past few years in Afghanistan is actually good news at this moment. A sound, properly resourced counterinsurgency has not failed in Afghanistan; it has never even been tried. So there is good reason to think that such a new strategy can succeed now. But we have to hurry, for as is often the case in these kinds of war, if you aren't winning, you're losing.

"The renewed and better resourced American effort in Afghanistan will, in time, produce a relatively stable and prosperous Central Asian state."

The United States Is Well Positioned to Win the War in Afghanistan

Peter Bergen

Peter Bergen is a senior fellow at the New America Foundation. In the following viewpoint, he argues that Afghanistan is not that violent compared with Iraq and wartime Vietnam, that the Taliban are relatively weak, that the Afghan people are relatively supportive of the international occupation, and that Afghanistan has a long history of stable statehood. For all these reasons, he concludes the Barack Obama administration's efforts in Afghanistan will lead to victory against the Taliban and a better future for Afghanistan.

Peter Bergen, "Winning the Good War: Why Afghanistan Is Not Obama's Vietnam," *Washington Monthly*, July–August 2009. Copyright © 2009 by Washington Monthly Publishing, LLC, 733 15th St. NW, Suite 520, Washington DC 20005. (202) 393-5155. www.washingtonmonthly.com. Reproduced by permission.

As you read, consider the following questions:

1. According to Bergen, what is the size of the Taliban force fighting the Americans, and how does this compare with the size of the insurgency movement that fought against the Soviets?

2. What percentage of Afghans voted in the 2004 president election, and how does this level of participation compare with American elections, according to Bergen?

3. Why does Bergen believe that more American soldiers in Afghanistan will reduce civilian casualties?

Throughout his campaign last year [in 2008], President Barack Obama said repeatedly that the real central front of the war against terrorists was on the Afghanistan-Pakistan border. And now [in summer 2009] he is living up to his campaign promise to roll back the Taliban and al-Qaeda [a terrorist organization] with significant resources. By the end of the year there will be some 70,000 American soldiers in Afghanistan, and the Obama administration is pushing for billions of dollars in additional aid to both Afghanistan and Pakistan.

Not Vietnam, Not Iraq

This has caused consternation among some in the Democratic Party. In May, fifty-one House Democrats voted against continued funding for the Afghan war. And David Obey, the chairman of the powerful House Appropriations Committee, which controls federal spending, says the White House must show concrete results in Afghanistan within a year—implying that if it doesn't do so, he will move to turn off the money spigot. If this is the attitude of Obama's own party, one can imagine what the Republicans will be saying if his "Af-Pak [Afghanistan-Pakistan]" strategy doesn't start yielding results as they gear up for the 2010 midterm elections.

It's not just politicians who are souring on the Afghan war. A *USA Today* poll earlier this year found that 42 percent of Americans believe the war is a mistake, up from 6 percent in 2002. The media has only added to the gloom. *Newsweek* ran a cover story in January speculating that Afghanistan could be Obama's Vietnam. And the *New York Times* has run prominent opinion pieces with headlines like "The 'Good War' Isn't Worth Fighting" and "Fearing Another Quagmire in Afghanistan."

But the growing skepticism about Obama's chances for success in Afghanistan is largely based on deep misreadings of both the country's history and the views of its people, which are often compounded by facile comparisons to the United States's misadventures of past decades in Southeast Asia and the Middle East. Afghanistan will not be Obama's Vietnam, nor will it be his Iraq. Rather, the renewed and better re-sourced American effort in Afghanistan will, in time, produce a relatively stable and prosperous Central Asian state.

Objections to Obama's ramp-up in Afghanistan begin with the observation that Afghanistan has long been the "graveyard of empires"—as went the disastrous British expedition there in 1842 and the Soviet invasion in 1979, so too the current American occupation is doomed to follow. In fact, any number of empire builders, from Alexander the Great to the Mogul emperor Babur in the sixteenth century to the British in the Second Afghan War three decades after their infamous defeat, have won military victories in Afghanistan. The graveyard of empires metaphor belongs in the graveyard of clichés.

The Soviets, of course, spent almost a decade waging war in Afghanistan, only to retreat ignominiously in 1989, an important factor in their own empire's consignment to history's dustbin [the Soviet Union collapsed in 1991]. But today's American-led intervention in Afghanistan is quite different from the Communist occupation. The Soviet army killed more than a million Afghans and forced some five million more to flee the country, creating what was then the world's largest refugee population. The Soviets also sowed millions of mines (including some that resembled toys), making Afghanistan one of the most heavily mined countries in the world. And Soviet soldiers were a largely unprofessional rabble of conscripts who drank heavily, used drugs, and consistently engaged in looting. The Soviets' strategy, tactics, and behavior were, in short, the exact opposite of those used in successful counterinsurgency campaigns.

Unsurprisingly, the brutal Soviet occupation provoked a countrywide insurrection that drew from a wide array of ethnic groups—Tajiks, Uzbeks, Pashtuns, and Hazaras—and every class in Afghan society, from mullahs [religious leaders] to urban professionals to peasants. By contrast, the insurgents in Afghanistan today are overwhelmingly rural Pashtuns [the main Taliban ethnic group] with negligible support in urban areas and among other ethnic groups.

That makes quite a difference to the scale of today's insurgency. Even the most generous estimates of the size of the Taliban force hold it to be no more than 20,000 men, while authoritative estimates of the numbers of Afghans on the battlefield at any given moment in the war against the Soviets range up to 250,000. The Taliban insurgency today is only around 10 percent the size of what the Soviets faced.

And while today's Afghan insurgents are well financed, in part by the drug trade, this backing is not on the scale of the financial and military support that the anti-Communist guerrillas enjoyed in the 1980s. The mujahideen [the name for the Islamic anti-Soviet fighters] were the recipients of billions of dollars of American and Saudi aid, large-scale Pakistani training, and sophisticated U.S. military hardware such as highly effective anti-aircraft Stinger missiles, which ended the Soviets' command of the air.

Afghanistan Is Governable

A corollary to the argument that Afghanistan is unconquerable is the argument that it is ungovernable—that the country has never been a functioning nation-state, and that its people, mired in a culture of violence not amenable to Western fixes, have no interest in helping to build a more open and peaceful society. Certainly endemic low-level warfare is embedded in Pashtun society—the words for cousin and enemy in Pashtu, for instance, are the same. But the level of violence in Afghanistan is actually far lower than most Americans believe. In 2008 more than 2,000 Afghan civilians died at the hands of the Taliban or coalition forces; this is too many, but it is also less than a quarter of the deaths last year in Iraq, a country that is both more sparsely populated and often assumed to be easier to govern. (At the height of the violence in Iraq, 3,200 civilians were dying *every month*, making the country around twenty times more violent than Afghanistan is today.) Not only are Afghan civilians much safer under American occupation than Iraqis, they are also statistically less likely to be killed in the war than anyone living in the United States during the early 1990s, when the U.S. murder rate peaked at more than 24,000 killings a year.

An assertion that deserves a similarly hard look is the argument that nation building in Afghanistan is doomed because the country isn't a nation-state, but rather a jury-rigged patchwork of competing tribal groupings. In fact, Afghanistan is a much older nation-state than, say, Italy or Germany, both of which were only unified in the late nineteenth century. Modern Afghanistan is considered to have emerged with the first Afghan empire under Ahmad Shah Durrani in 1747, and so has been a nation for decades longer than the United States. Accordingly, Afghans have a strong sense of nationhood.

What they have had just as long, however, is a weak central state. The last king of Afghanistan, Zahir Shah, who reigned from 1933 to 1973, presided lightly over a country in a time that Afghans recall with great nostalgia as one of relative peace and prosperity. Today President Hamid Karzai similarly presides over a weak central government. Critics contend that President Karzai is unable or unwilling to fight the epic corruption in his government, and joke that he is only the "mayor of Kabul [capital of Afghanistan]." This criticism is largely accurate, but misses the fact that Karzai is still a somewhat popular leader in Afghanistan. Fifty-two percent of Afghans say that the president is doing a good job, only 15 percent less than the number of Americans who say the same thing about Obama—and that is eight years after Karzai assumed the leadership of a country in which any honeymoon period has long since evaporated. Afghans are also wildly enthusiastic about participating in real politics. In the 2004 presidential election, more than 80 percent of them turned out to vote, an accomplishment Americans haven't been able to claim since the late nineteenth century.

So if Afghanistan itself is not necessarily ungovernable, what of the other argument—that as far as the United States is concerned, the war there will be a rerun of Vietnam? Hardly. The similarities between the Taliban and the Vietcong end with their mutual hostility toward the U.S. military. The some 20,000 Taliban fighters are too few to hold even small Afghan towns, let alone mount a Tet-style offensive on Kabul.[1] As a military force, they are armed lightly enough to constitute a tactical problem, not a strategic threat. By contrast, the Vietcong and the North Vietnamese Army at the height of the Vietnam War numbered more than half a million men who were equipped with artillery and tanks, and were well supplied by both the Soviet Union and Mao's China [that is, by Mao Tse Tung's China]. And the number of casualties is orders of magnitude smaller: in Afghanistan last year [2008],

---

1. The Tet offensive was a massive assault launched by North Vietnamese forces on the forces of the United States and South Vietnam in 1968.

154 American soldiers died, the largest number since the fall of the Taliban; in 1968, the deadliest year of the Vietnam conflict, the same number of U.S. servicemen were dying *every four days*. Estimates of the total civilian death toll in Vietnam are in the low millions, while estimates of the total number of Afghan civilian casualties since the fall of the Taliban are in the thousands.

Nor has the U.S. intervention in Afghanistan been anywhere near as expensive as Vietnam was—in fact, that's in part why American efforts have not met with as much success as they could have. During the Vietnam War, the United States spent almost 10 percent of its GDP [gross domestic product] on military spending. Today's military expenditures are somewhere between 4 and 5 percent of GDP, and of that, Afghanistan last year consumed only 6 percent of the total expenditure, while Iraq sucked up some five times that amount. And unlike the Vietnamese and Iraqis, Afghans have generally embraced international forces. In 2005, four years after the fall of the Taliban, eight out of ten Afghans expressed in a BBC/ABC poll a favorable opinion of the United States, and the same number supported foreign soldiers in their country. Contrast that with Iraq, where a BBC/ABC poll in 2005 found that only one in three Iraqis supported international forces in their country. While the same poll taken in Afghanistan this year reported, for the first time, that just under half of Afghans have a favorable view of the United States, that's still a higher approval rating than the U.S. gets in any other Muslim-majority country save Lebanon. And a solid majority of Afghans continue to approve of the international forces in their country. What Afghans want is not for American and other foreign soldiers to leave, but for them to deliver on their promises of helping to midwife a more secure and prosperous country.

Abandoning Afghanistan Will Not Work

Skeptics of Obama's Afghanistan policy say that the right approach is to either reduce American commitments there or just get out entirely. The short explanation of why this won't work is that the United States has tried this already—twice. In 1989, after the most successful covert program in the history of the CIA [Central Intelligence Agency] helped to defeat the Soviets in Afghanistan, the George H. W. Bush administration closed the U.S. embassy in Kabul. The Clinton administration subsequently effectively zeroed out aid to the country, one of the poorest in the world. Out of the chaos of the Afghan civil war in the early 1990s emerged the Taliban, who then gave sanctuary to al Qaeda. In 2001, the next Bush administration [of George W. Bush] returned to topple the Taliban, but because of its ideological aversion to nation building it ensured that Afghanistan was the least-resourced per capita reconstruction effort the United States has engaged in since World War II. An indication of how desultory those efforts were was the puny size of the Afghan army, which two years after the fall of the Taliban numbered only 5,000 men, around the same size as the police department of an American city like Houston. We got what we paid for with this on-the-cheap approach: since 2001 the Taliban has reemerged, and fused ideologically and tactically with al-Qaeda. The new Taliban has adopted wholesale al-Qaeda's Iraq playbook of suicide attacks, IED [improvised explosive devices] operations, hostage beheadings, and aggressive video-based information campaigns. (The pre-9/11 Taliban had, of course, banned television.)

Why should we believe that the alternative offered by the Obama administration—committing large numbers of boots on the ground and significant sums of money to Afghanistan—has a better chance of success? In part, because the Afghan people themselves, the center of gravity in a counterinsurgency, are rooting for us to win. BBC/ABC polling found that 58 percent of Afghans named the Taliban—who only 7 percent of Afghans view favorably—as the greatest threat to their nation; only 8 percent said it was the United States.

There are other positive indices. Refugees don't return to places they don't think have a future, and more than four million Afghan refugees have returned home since the fall of the Taliban. (By contrast, about the same number of Iraqi refugees fled their homes after the American-led invasion of their country in 2003, and few have returned.) There are also more than two million Afghan kids in schools, including, of course, many girls. Music, kites, movies, independent newspapers, and TV stations—all of which were banned under the Taliban—are now ubiquitous. One in six Afghans now has a cell phone, in a country that didn't have a phone system under the Taliban. And, according to the World Bank, the 2007 GDP growth rate for Afghanistan was 14 percent. Under Taliban rule the country was so poor that the World Bank didn't even bother to measure its economic indicators.

Today 40 percent of Afghans say their country is going in the right direction (only 17 percent of Americans felt the same way in the waning months of the [George W.] Bush administration). Considering Afghanistan's rampant drug trade, pervasive corruption, and rising violence, this may seem counterintuitive—until you recall that no country in the world has ever suffered Afghanistan's combination of an invasion and occupation by a totalitarian regime followed by a civil war, with subsequent "government" by warlords and then the neo-medieval misrule of the Taliban. In other words, the bar is pretty low. No Afghan is expecting that the country will turn into, say, Belgium, but there is an expectation that Afghanistan can be returned to the somewhat secure condition it enjoyed in the 1970s before the Soviet invasion, and that the country will be able to grow its way out of being simply a subsistence agricultural economy.

Obama's Afghanistan strategy is well poised to deliver on these expectations because it primarily emphasizes increased security for the Afghan people—the first public good that Afghans want. In the south of Afghanistan, where the insurgency is the most intense, the U.S. is deploying two Marine brigades and a Stryker brigade, 17,000 soldiers in all, to supplement the thinly stretched British, Dutch, and Canadian forces in the region. These are not the kind of units that do peacekeeping; they will go in and clear areas of the Taliban and, most crucially, hold them. This will be a major improvement in a region where NATO [North Atlantic Treaty Organization] forces have often had enough manpower to clear areas but not to hold them. One Western diplomat in Kabul joked grimly to me that every year in the south NATO soldiers have gone in to "mow the lawn." This time the idea is not to let the grass grow back.

One potential objection to Obama's Afghanistan strategy is that the thousands of additional American soldiers that are now deploying to the country will only be the thin end of the wedge, because the Pentagon will inevitably ask for significantly more troops. This is a reasonable concern, but should be obviated by the fact that dramatically scaling up the size of the Afghan army and police is the best American exit strategy from the country, and that effort is at the heart of Obama's plan.

Today there are only some 160,000 Afghan soldiers and cops, a quarter of the size of Iraq's security services, and they are tasked with bringing order to a country that is larger and more populous than Iraq. Obama wants to modestly improve the size and professionalism of Afghanistan's police force, and almost double the ranks of the Afghan army over the next two years. The latter is especially important because Afghans trust their army more than any other institution, and the army has emerged as a truly national force not riven by ethnic divisions. To help train those Afghan security services, some 4,000 trainers from the 82nd Airborne are deploying to Afghanistan. The administration is also pushing to make salaries in those forces competitive with what the Taliban pays its foot soldiers—often three times what an Afghan policeman makes.

Civilian Casualties and Opium

Another possible objection to the introduction of more U.S. soldiers into Afghanistan is that, inevitably, they will kill more civilians, the main issue that angers Afghans about the foreign military presence. In fact, the presence of more boots on the ground is likely to *reduce* civilian casualties, because historically it has been the overreliance on American air strikes—as a result of too few ground forces—which has been the key cause of civilian deaths. According to the U.S. Air Force, between January and August 2008 there were almost 2,400 air strikes in Afghanistan, fully three times as many as in Iraq. And the United Nations concluded that it was air strikes, rather than action on the ground, which were responsible for the largest percentage—64 percent—of civilian deaths attributed to pro-government forces in 2008.

Cognizant of the importance of the issue of civilian casualties, in his Senate confirmation hearing in June the new commander in Afghanistan, Lt. Gen. Stanley McChrystal, testified that their avoidance "may be the critical point" of American military operations, adding, "I cannot overstate my commitment to the importance of this concept." McChrystal, generally regarded as one of the most effective officers of his generation, has now put the avoidance of civilian casualties at the core of his military strategy in Afghanistan, and that message will undoubtedly filter down the chain of command.

These key features of the Obama administration's Afghan policy are supplemented by several others that merit highlighting and represent a distinct break from the Bush administration's sputtering efforts. One is a shifting emphasis within the attempt to curtail the opium trade, from poppy eradication to going after the drug lords. This is a no-brainer—poppy eradication penalizes poor Afghan farmers

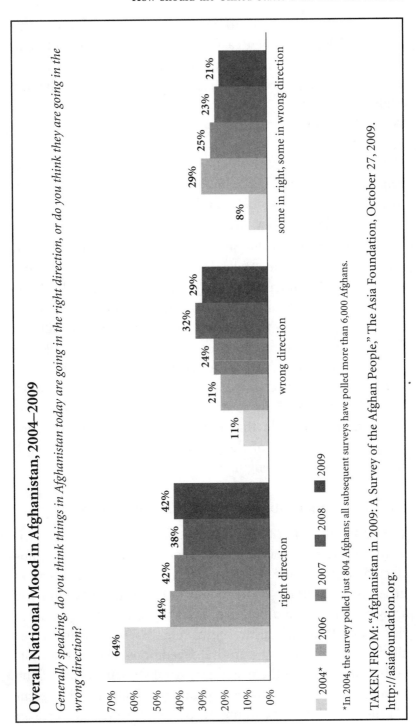

Overall National Mood in Afghanistan, 2004–2009

Generally speaking, do you think things in Afghanistan today are going in the right direction, or do you think they are going in the wrong direction?

right direction
- 2004*: 64%
- 2006: 44%
- 2007: 42%
- 2008: 38%
- 2009: 42%

wrong direction
- 2004*: 11%
- 2006: 21%
- 2007: 24%
- 2008: 32%
- 2009: 29%

some in right, some in wrong direction
- 2004*: 8%
- 2006: 29%
- 2007: 25%
- 2008: 23%
- 2009: 21%

2004*   2006   2007   2008   2009

*In 2004, the survey polled just 804 Afghans; all subsequent surveys have polled more than 6,000 Afghans.

TAKEN FROM: "Afghanistan in 2009: A Survey of the Afghan People," The Asia Foundation, October 27, 2009. http://asiafoundation.org.

who can't pay the bribes to ensure their fields are not eradicated, and who are then easy marks for Taliban recruitment. Obama is also seeking to draw in potential regional partners like Iran, which played a vital role in the formation of the first Afghan government that emerged out of the discussions in Bonn [Germany] in the winter of 2001. And third, the U.S. government plans to regularly host meetings among key Afghan and Pakistani officials, as it did in Washington [D.C.] in February and May. This is important for confidence-building measures between Afghans and Pakistanis, whose relations have varied between icy and openly hostile.

This brings us to the one skunk at this garden party, and it is a rather large one: Afghanistan's nuclear-armed, al-Qaeda- and Taliban-headquartering neighbor to the east. The Pakistani dimension of Obama's Af-Pak strategy is his critics' most reasonable objection to his plans for the region. It is difficult for the United States to have an effective strategy for Pakistan when *Pakistan* doesn't have an effective strategy for Pakistan. There is a set of interwoven problems that the country must face if it is to effectively confront the militants in its own territory. If it fails to do this, the regional insurgency that encompasses both sides of the Afghanistan/Pakistan border will continue to gather strength.

Pakistan, the Taliban, and the United States

The first problem is that Pakistan effectively has two governments. There is a weak, elected civilian one, and a strong, unelected military one. Pakistan's civilian government knows little about military strategy and is often at odds with the army, which has veto power over all aspects of national security policy. Pakistan's army, meanwhile, has wavered ineffectually between mounting punitive expeditions against the militants and appeasing them, and is generally unable or unwilling to adopt an effective strategy against the Taliban. (The recent [April–May 2009] operations in the Swat Valley [an area in northwest Pakistan], characterized by the use of artillery and air power and millions of refugees streaming out of the battle zone, are not the hallmarks of a successful counterinsurgency.) As a result, civilians caught in the middle don't know which way the wind will blow from day to day. They have reason to be skeptical that the government will protect them from the predations of the Taliban if the former chooses to revisit the various "peace" agreements it has struck with the militants over the past several years. Finally, the Pakistani establishment has done a poor job of persuading the public that the Taliban and other militant groups to which it once gave succor, and which are now attacking the Pakistani state, pose a grave threat to Pakistan itself.

Some have argued that if the U.S. does succeed in Afghanistan, it will only make this situation worse, pushing the Taliban and their allied foreign fighters into Pakistan and further destabilizing the already rickety nuclear-armed state. But this line of reasoning has the equation precisely the wrong way around: al-Qaeda was founded in Pakistan in 1988, and many of the Taliban's leaders and foot soldiers emerged out of Pakistani madrassas [religious schools] and refugee camps. Following the vacuum created by the Afghan civil war of the early 1990s, the Pakistan-based militants expanded into Afghanistan. The notion of the militants enjoying safe havens in either Afghanistan or Pakistan is a false choice—in truth, they have had a persistent presence in both countries for decades.

That said, there are some hopeful signs that the militants have shot themselves in the feet in Pakistan. There has been no single "9/11 moment [referring to the September 11, 2001, terrorist attacks on the United States]" but the cumulative weight of a number of events—the Taliban's assassination of Benazir Bhutto [a Pakistani politician and opposition leader assassinated shortly before the Pakistani elections of 2008]; al-Qaeda's bombing of the Marriott hotel in Islamabad [capital of Pakistan]; the attacks on the visiting Sri Lankan cricket team and the police academy in Lahore; the widely circulated video images of the Taliban flogging a seventeen-year-old girl; and the Taliban's decision to move from Swat into Buner District, only sixty miles from Islamabad—[all events in 2008–2009] has accomplished something similar. Each of these incidents has provoked revulsion and fear among the Pakistani public. Indicative of this, the alliance of pro-Taliban religious parties known as the MMA was annihilated in the 2008 election, earning just 2 percent of the vote. And support for suicide bombing among Pakistanis has cratered, from 33 percent in 2002 to 5 percent in 2008.

The United States can neither precipitously withdraw from Afghanistan nor help foster the emergence of a stable Afghan state by doing it on the cheap; the consequence would be the return of the Taliban and al-Qaeda. Fortunately, the U.S. is not alone; unlike in Iraq, there is an international coalition of forty-two countries in Afghanistan supporting NATO efforts there, with troops or other assistance. Even Muslim countries are part of this mix. Turkey, for instance, ran the International Security Assistance Force in Afghanistan in 2005, and the United Arab Emirates and Jordan have both sent small numbers of soldiers.

The United States overthrew the Taliban in the winter of 2001. It has a moral obligation to ensure that when it does leave Afghanistan it does so secure in the knowledge that the country will never again be a launching pad for the world's deadliest terrorist groups, and that the country is on the way to a measure of stability and prosperity. When that happens, it is not too fanciful to think that Afghanistan's majestic mountains, verdant valleys, and jasmine-scented gardens may once again draw the tourists that once flocked there.

| "The question is not whether we will negotiate with the Taliban, but when, under what circumstances, and with which members?"

America Must Negotiate with the Taliban

Andrew Blandford

Andrew Blandford is a joint degree student at Harvard Law School and the Harvard Kennedy School of Government focusing on international law and international relations. In the following viewpoint, he argues that total victory over the Taliban in Afghanistan is unlikely. Therefore, he says, negotiation with the Taliban, or with some factions of the Taliban, will be necessary to bring the war to an end, unless the United States simply decides to withdraw. Blandford suggests that America should wait to negotiate until its overall position in the country is improved, but he concludes that negotiations eventually will be necessary and beneficial.

As you read, consider the following questions:

1. According to Blandford, what conditions do the Taliban say must be fulfilled before they are willing to negotiate?

Andrew Blandford, "Talking with the Taliban: Should the U.S. 'Bargain with the Devil' in Afghanistan?" *Harvard Negotiation Law Review*, 2009. Reproduced by permission.

2. What does Blandford say are the Taliban's two main interests?

3. What indirect costs does Blandford say the Barack Obama administration may incur by negotiating with the Taliban?

It is essential to begin conducting a sober analysis of whether the benefits of negotiating with the Taliban outweigh the costs. While there are many negotiations relevant to the Afghan War—between the U.S. and its NATO [North Atlantic Treaty Organization] allies, between the U.S. and the Afghan and Pakistani governments, and between the Pakistanis and the Taliban—this paper will focus on whether the United States, together with its allies in Kabul [the capital of Afghanistan] or NATO, should negotiate with the Taliban.

Conditions for Negotiations

As President [Barack] Obama orders more troops to Afghanistan [in 2009], the Taliban are making strategic gains in both Afghanistan and Pakistan. In February, even while U.S. drones stepped up attacks on Al-Qaeda [a terrorist group] and Taliban militants in the tribal areas in northwestern Pakistan, the Taliban effectively subdued the Pakistani military in the Swat Valley [a northwestern territory in Pakistan]. This demoralizing defeat prompted Islamabad [the capital of Pakistan] to negotiate an agreement with the Taliban, effectively ceding a large swath of territory in central Pakistan, allowing the Taliban to impose Sharia [Islamic] law and institute measures that included closing girls' schools, banning music, and installing "complaint boxes for reports of anti-Islamic behavior."

Even so, preliminary talks between the Afghan government and the Taliban have also taken place, albeit indirectly. But the Taliban claim that they will refuse to negotiate until all foreign forces are withdrawn from Afghanistan. Meanwhile, a State Department spokesman indicated that the [Afghan President

Hamid] Karzai government had set its own conditions that reportedly included "a renunciation of violence, acceptance of Afghanistan's democratic Constitution and a repudiation of Al Qaeda—all terms the Taliban leadership has rejected." Another State Department official referred to preconditions including the exclusion from talks of any member of the Taliban linked to 9-11 [the September 11, 2001, terrorist attacks on the United States] and the exclusion from the agenda of proposals concerning power sharing or land swaps.

Into this morass of positional bargaining now steps Richard Holbrooke, a veteran diplomat and President [Bill] Clinton's chief negotiator during the Bosnian War [of the 1990s]. In contrast to his mediation in Bosnia, his "Afpak [Afghanistan and Pakistan]" assignment promises a new breed of interlocutors: a loose coalition of Taliban and other militant groups, operating largely behind the Pakistani border, and perhaps unwilling or unable to implement any long-term agreement. With so much uncertainty, how to decide whether to negotiate with the Taliban? . . .

In Afghanistan the U.S. is interested primarily in maintaining its own security at the lowest possible cost in blood and treasure. Related interests include setting a strong precedent in the wider fight against terrorism, and providing for the development of Afghanistan in a manner that improves America's international standing and minimizes the risk that Afghanistan later backslides into a failed state.

The Taliban, too, have relatively simple interests. First, they have a strong interest in survival—as an organization and as individuals. Second, the Taliban and its members have an interest in retaining influence and prosperity following the ultimate withdrawal of foreign forces. This interest in power extends to a financial interest and an interest in good public relations.

Possible Outcomes

Since the parties already find themselves in the midst of war, the basic alternatives to a negotiated agreement are the continuation of war or an American withdrawal. Theoretically, the Taliban could surrender or be destroyed, but these outcomes seem relatively unlikely; as General [David] Petraeus has noted, "You don't kill or capture your way out of an industrial strength insurgency." It would seem that time is on the side of the Taliban regarding BATNAs,[1] as no foreign power has ever successfully maintained control of Afghanistan or imposed central rule.

To improve its BATNA, the U.S. must fill the power and legitimacy vacuum in Afghanistan in which President Karzai is essentially reduced to the role of the corrupt "mayor of Kabul." Before the U.S. withdraws under any scenario, the power of the Kabul government must be increased, warlords must be supported, or regional powers must step in to fill the vacuum. Clearly, the most acceptable alternative is to empower Kabul to legitimately govern the country as a whole, but it remains to be seen if this will be possible.

It appears that a ZOPA ["zone of possible agreement"; that is, a basis for agreement] will emerge only when the Obama administration determines that the security and international standing of the U.S. would not be unduly threatened by allowing a critical mass of "reconcilable" Taliban members to maintain some measure of power in Afghanistan. Determining whether U.S. security and reputational interests would be unduly threatened by such a negotiated outcome entails a balancing test between those interests and the administrations' other interests, including financial and domestic political interests.

The extent of both the critical mass of Taliban reconcilables and the power that they maintain depends largely on the

---

1. BATNA in negotiation theory is the "best alternative to a negotiated agreement." It refers to the course of action that will be taken if no negotiated solution is reached.

parties' evaluation of their BATNAs at the time of the negotiation. If negotiations were to occur now, President Obama would be playing with a weak hand. The Taliban's recent gains, the ubiquitous perception of the incompetence and corruption of the Karzai administration, and the worldwide financial crisis all signal that the Taliban's BATNA is superior to that of the U.S. and its allies. If it were to set an early deadline for a negotiated agreement with the Taliban, the U.S. could expect to obtain little more than a "decent interval" between a withdrawal and Taliban recidivism—perhaps by providing sanctuary to Al-Qaeda or denying women education and medical care. Significantly, the U.S. would probably have to offer the Taliban some degree of autonomy from Afghanistan's central government.

However, if negotiations were to occur (or continue) beyond a short-term time horizon, the U.S. could potentially change the game by improving its BATNA and reducing the attractiveness of the Taliban's BATNA. Under such negotiating circumstances, the U.S. may succeed in splitting off a critical mass of "reconcilables"—i.e. dissident Pashtuns [an ethnic group from which most Taliban support is drawn] affiliated with the Taliban—from the "irreconcilables"—a core of extremist ideologues. Theoretically, if this "divide and conquer" strategy were to work, the U.S. may need only "conquer" the irreconcilables, while paying off the reconcilable Pashtuns. . . .

Implementing an Agreement

Even if the Obama administration could negotiate a satisfactory agreement with the Taliban members it determined to be reconcilables, there is reason to doubt whether such an agreement could be implemented in Afghanistan. For example, *New York Times* correspondent Dexter Filkins explains that while Iraq is still a tribal society in which "a big bag of money" given to a tribal leader can effectively "deliver the tribe," Afghanistan is a country that "has been at war for thirty years and has been decimated and atomized—old tribal networks have been completely attenuated." Similarly, Noah Feldman argues that, in contrast to the Iraqi tribal structure which was built by the British to deliver patronage, "Afghanistan's tribes—a term that covers everything from large confederations to cousin-networks and extended families—are not natural vehicles for creating loyalty to a central government." . . .

The fissures [between Afghan groups] of most direct relevance to the issue of implementation are those within the Taliban reconcilables themselves. Is there anyone who can speak for the reconcilables as a whole and deliver their compliance with a negotiated agreement? At the very least, this hypothetical representative would have to be free of any direct link to the September 11 attacks.

The recent Pakistan-Taliban ceasefire agreement in Swat—evidently unacceptable in substance—also provides an example of the procedural challenges involved in attempting to peel reconcilables away from irreconcilables. There, the Pakistani government brokered the cease-fire agreement "with an aging Islamic leader, Maulana Sufi Muhammad," viewing the negotiation "as a way to separate what it considered to be more approachable militants, like Muhammad, from hard-line Taliban leaders like Maulana Fazlullah, his son-in-law." Thus far, it appears that the Taliban have not implemented the terms of this agreement.

In addition to the potential benefits of a negotiated agreement relative to the parties' BATNA, it is also necessary to calculate the costs "incurred by the negotiation process itself, regardless of whether a deal is ultimately made." Since the U.S.'s BATNA is extremely unappealing, the costs of negotiating must reach a very high threshold to rule out negotiations. . . .

The direct costs of negotiating with the Taliban reconcilables include the time, money, and manpower spent in seeking out—perhaps even helping to consolidate—and then negotiating with the reconcilables. Even if Mr. Holbrooke is granted sufficient latitude to avoid conferring routinely with an overworked administration, presumably there are opportunity costs [that is, there are costs to spending resources on Afghan negotiations rather than using those resources for other things] to pursuing a strategy of negotiation with the Taliban—as opposed to having his team focus on working with Pakistan, NATO allies, or the Afghan government. Direct costs would also include any information that may be disclosed to the Taliban during the negotiation. For example, if there were an American presence at the negotiating table while the U.S.'s BATNA remained unattractive, the Taliban may perceive that the U.S. has been weakened and ready to withdraw.

The indirect costs of negotiating with the Taliban reconcilables include the signal it may send "behind the table" to U.S. allies and domestic constituents. If the Obama administration were to walk out on the negotiations, it may then face increased difficulty in convincing its allies and its constituents of the necessity to continue the war well into the future. In negotiating with the Taliban, the U.S. may also have to incur the indirect cost of setting a precedent that the U.S. will now "negotiate with terrorists." To minimize this cost, the Obama administration could initiate negotiations secretly and ultimately rebrand its negotiation partners as "reconcilables," "Pashtun rebels," or Taliban "affiliates." Also, as a toppled government, the Taliban may be distinguishable from, for example, hijackers, or purely non-state actors such as Al-Qaeda.

The Morality of Negotiations

Closely related to the indirect costs of the negotiation process are questions of legitimacy and morality. [Robert H.] Mnookin and [Gabriella] Blum note that "[p]roviding a counterpart with 'a place at the table' acknowledges their existence, and (to some degree) the validity of their interests and claims." The U.S. may indeed find it necessary to acknowledge the validity of the interests of some Pashtuns who have seen their relatives killed and property destroyed during the war, but it should be able to distinguish these cases from the extremism of the Taliban ideology. Alternatively, the U.S. could negotiate entirely through the Afghan government or try to keep its role secret.

A related concern is avoiding the perception that the U.S. is rewarding past bad behavior. But, in the words of [Israeli politician] Yitzhak Rabin, "You don't make peace with friends, you make peace with very unsavory enemies"—enemies that have necessarily engaged in bad behavior in waging war against you. Presumably, few states will emulate the Taliban in providing safe haven to terrorists simply because the U.S. may be expected to negotiate after seven years of war.

The U.S. must pursue numerous strategies if it is to fulfill its objectives in Afghanistan: it must convince Pakistan to increase its pressure on the Taliban in the tribal areas, compel NATO allies to dedicate more troops to Afghanistan, and build the capacity of the Afghan government to provide much-needed services to its people in order to lure them back from the appeal of authoritarian stability. These strategies are not alternatives to a negotiated agreement, but rather complements to negotiating with the reconcilables. Barring total victory for the U.S. over a pervasive, locally-based force, the question is not *whether* we will negotiate with the Taliban, but *when, under what circumstances,* and *with which members?* It may indeed be too soon to push for direct talks with the Taliban because the conditions are not yet ripe to negotiate an acceptable outcome for the U.S., and serious costs may result. But it is probably never too soon for indirect talks, in order to feel out the Taliban's interests and seek a path to a ZOPA—all while striving to increase bargaining power by improving the U.S.'s BATNA and decreasing the attractiveness of the Taliban's BATNA.

"By supporting negotiations, we would be awarding the extremists a victory that they could not otherwise win. Why legitimize something that is opposed by 90% of the population?"

America Should Not Negotiate with the Taliban

Inge Fryklund

Inge Fryklund is an international development consultant who has worked on governance in Afghanistan, Iraq, Kosovo, the West Bank, and Tajikistan. In the following viewpoint, she argues that the Taliban have little popular support, and that negotiating with them would simply grant them legitimacy. The only reason the Taliban are able to survive is, she says, because of the failure and corruption of Afghanistan's central government, which has too much power. She concludes that decentralizing the government could make local government more effective, which would undermine the Taliban without any need for negotiation.

As you read, consider the following questions:

1. According to Fryklund, why is the Hamid Karzai government interested in negotiations?

Inge Fryklund, "Don't Negotiate with the Taliban," *Foreign Policy in Focus*, December 31, 2009. Copyright © 2009 Institute for Policy Studies. Reproduced by permission.

2. Why does Fryklund say that it is in the interest of Afghan government officials to create and maintain convoluted requirements?

3. What is the IDLG and what does Frylunk say its mission is?

The Afghan problem can't be addressed, let alone solved, by force. Nor can it be solved through negotiations between the Afghan government and the Taliban. The conflict, after all, is not between two distinct segments of the population. Negotiation is an appropriate strategy when there is indeed a two-party conflict—as in a civil war—and both sides have support among different factions of the population. But neither the government nor the Taliban has much popular support. The problem is not the presence of the Taliban; it's the absence of good governance. Negotiation and force are not just unproductive strategies; they are strategies addressing the wrong problem.

The Taliban Have Little Support

During my $3\frac{1}{2}$ years spent in Afghanistan working as a contractor for the UN [United Nations] Development Program and with the U.S. Agency for International Development, I heard the figure 10% for the proportion of the population actually supporting the extremist social views of the Taliban. From my contact with Afghan citizens—as well as my work with the judiciary, district officials, and provincial representatives of the line ministries—I'd second this assessment. The Taliban are not a group with an independent constituency among the population. They are the beneficiaries of governance failure, a symptom of the problem, not its cause.

By supporting negotiations, we would be awarding the extremists a victory that they could not otherwise win. Why legitimize something that is opposed by 90% of the population? The [Afghan President Hamid] Karzai government is similarly interested in negotiations; Western support for the idea anoints the corrupt central government as a legitimate party to negotiation. Again, the interests of the vast majority of the Afghan population are ignored.

Neither would negotiation serve U.S. interests in the long run. A Western-sponsored division of the spoils between the corrupt central government and the vicious Taliban does nothing to resolve the underlying governance problems that the average Afghan struggles against. When neither government nor Taliban has much popular support, a deal between the two would only set the stage for a new blow-up a year or two down the road—when the United States would have less credibility, many fewer options, and less public support for intervention.

Change the Governance Structure

Governance really does matter, and the key is accountability to local citizens. Afghanistan has a highly centralized governance structure. The Afghan president appoints all governors, district officials, and mayors, and he can dismiss or transfer them on a whim. Last year, in a lecture at American University in Kabul [the capital of Afghanistan], an Afghan-American professor identified this extreme centralization as the root problem in Afghanistan. He said Afghans aren't citizens; they are subjects. This drew wild applause from the Afghan audience.

This centralized structure fosters corruption. All the incentives are perverse. Would-be appointees and employees may have to pay (in cash or other services) to obtain their positions. They expect to recoup their investment by extracting bribes and fees from the hapless citizens. Governmental employees have an open-ended profit-making opportunity, and citizens are without recourse. Americans with a corrupt or incompetent mayor can vote him out—and the threat acts as a check on behavior between elections. Afghans have no such option.

It is in the interests of Afghan government officials to create and maintain convoluted requirements, e.g., for getting a business license or recording a land deed. Every signature required presents an extortion opportunity. This puts a damper on business activity. A business that has to stay under the radar can never grow. With a more business-friendly environment, economic growth would be possible, reducing incentives for young men to sign on with the Taliban for the paycheck.

The U.S. State Department has the right impulse in trying to identify and support the more effective local governments, but this assumes a governance structure in which local government has both permanence and incentives to be responsive. Good government occasionally occurs, but it is only due to conscientious individuals, not to incentives inherent in the governance structure. Some officials, such as Governor [Gulab] Mangal in Helmand, are indeed talented and committed. However, it is largely a waste of tax dollars to invest in officials who could be removed tomorrow.

Decentralize

Afghanistan does indeed have a "unitary" (as opposed to a federal) system of government, but this does not preclude locally chosen government with real powers. A significant decentralization of power, responsibility and accountability does not require any change to the Constitution or the convening of a Loya Jirga [an Afghan grand council, convened to discuss issues of national importance]. It only requires statutory change.

The U.S. government should use whatever leverage it has to get laws and practices changed in order for Afghanistan to implement accountable local government. This can be done immediately. Change does not require a five-year transition as suggested by the Afghan Independent Directorate of Local Government (IDLG)—a contradiction in terms if there ever was one. This is a unit of the central government, established in mid 2007 when the local government supervision section of the Ministry of the Interior was spun off. While it may appear to donors that something is being done to increase local accountability, IDLG's mission remains one of "supervising" local government, not decentralizing it. If, however, local officials were locally selected, were responsible for spending decisions, and had an incentive to serve the taxpayers, such locally directed technical assistance could be highly effective.

Why should Afghans (and donors) have to settle for working around a dysfunctional governance structure that fosters corruption and is unable to deliver services? Let's address the underlying accountability problem. With responsive local government, support for the Taliban would melt away and there would be no reason to negotiate with the hard-core remnants.

Periodical Bibliography

The following articles have been selected to supplement the diverse views presented in this chapter.

Con Coughlin "We Will Never Defeat the Taliban if They Think We're Going Home," *Telegraph*, May 27, 2010.

Thomas McAdams Deford "Afghanistan: Our Vital National Interest, at Least for the Next 18 Months," *The Free Press*, December 3, 2009.

Karen DeYoung "British Official Urges Afghanistan to Negotiate with Taliban, Other Insurgents," *Washington Post*, March 11, 2010.

Frederick W. Kagan and Kimberly Kagan "Why Negotiate with the Taliban?" *Wall Street Journal*, March 16, 2010.

Los Angeles Times "Dust-Up: Does the U.S. Have a Vital National Interest in Afghanistan Anymore?" September 23, 2009.

Andrew C. McCarthy "A Dangerous Delusion," *National Review Online*, September 4, 2009.

Greg Mills "Kandahar Through the Taliban's Eyes," *Foreign Policy*, May 27, 2010.

OilPrice.com "Interests in Afghanistan and Pakistan Set to Collide, with Global Implications," December 30, 2009.

Howard Portnoy "U.S. Death Toll in Afghanistan Reaches 1,000," Examiner.com, May 28, 2010.

Paul Starobin "Time to Talk to the Taliban?" *National Security*, May 17, 2010.

What Is the Taliban's Relationship with Pakistan?

Chapter Preface

Benazir Bhutto, former prime minister of Pakistan, was assassinated in 2007 after departing a political rally two
weeks before the scheduled Pakistani general election of 2008,
in which she was a leading opposition candidate. Her death,
which has been linked to Taliban radicals, painfully high-
lighted Pakistan's struggles with security and Islamic fundamentalism.

Bhutto had a long history in Pakistani politics. In the early
1970s her father was the Pakistani prime minister. She herself
was prime minister twice, from 1988 to 1990 and 1993 to
1996. Both times she was removed from office on charges of
corruption. She left the country in 1999, but returned in 2007
after being granted an amnesty for corruption charges by Pervez Musharraf, head of the military regime of Pakistan. When
she was killed, she was running in a parliamentary election
that, it was hoped, had the potential to shift Pakistan back toward civilian rule. "Western powers saw in her a popular leader
with liberal leanings who could bring much needed legitimacy" to the fight against terrorism, according to a December
27, 2007, obituary on the *BBC News* Web site.

Bhutto's liberalism, her ties to the West, and the power-
sharing deal she made with Musharraf, however, made her a
target for fundamentalist elements in Pakistan. Massoud An-
sari writing in the *Telegraph* on October 7, 2007, noted that a
Taliban leader "declared that suicide bombers would launch
attacks on Ms Bhutto as soon as she returned." In fact, "A terror attack targeting [Bhutto's] motorcade in Karachi killed 136
people on the day she returned to Pakistan after eight years of
self-imposed exile," according to a December 27, 2007, article
on CNN.com/asia. Bhutto, however, escaped that attempt on
her life.

On December 27, 2007, Bhutto addressed a political rally in the city of Rawalpindi, Punjab, Pakistan. While leaving the rally in her car, she was shot, and a bomb exploded near her car. She and twenty-three other people were killed.

Who assassinated Bhutto remains unclear. "Pakistan's government and the CIA [Central Intelligence Agency] blamed the killing on Baitullah Mehsud, a top Pakistani Taliban leader with ties to al Qaeda," according to an April 16, 2010, article on CNN.com. However, a United Nations investigation also reprimanded the government of Pakistan, which was then controlled by Musharraf. The investigation censured the government for "not providing adequate security to Ms. Bhutto despite knowing the threats that she faced, and for impeding the investigation into the causes of her death," according to Huma Imtiaz writing on April 14, 2010, on the *Foreign Policy* Web site.

The mix of violence, Islamic extremism, official confusion, and possible corruption that resulted in Bhutto's assassination throw into relief the conditions that make confronting the Taliban in Pakistan so difficult. The following viewpoints present different perspectives on the best ways to manage these problems, as well as how to deal with the Pakistani Taliban.

"[Pakistan] President Asif Zardari has repeatedly declared the war against [extremists] a war for Pakistan's soul."

Pakistan Opposes the Taliban

Husain Haqqani

Husain Haqqani is Pakistan's ambassador to the United States. In the following viewpoint, he argues that while Pakistan's former governments were not as committed as they should have been to fighting the Taliban, the current democratic government is determined to defeat the insurgents in the Swat Valley and throughout the country. He says Pakistan needs military and economic aid from the United States, and that such aid will help Pakistan to defeat the Taliban and to become a moderate, modern Islamic state.

As you read, consider the following questions:

1. According to Haqqani, the international community panicked when the Taliban took which town, which is located where?

2. What did the agreement in the Swat Valley entail, according to Haqqani?

Husain Haqqani, "How Pakistan Is Countering the Taliban," *Wall Street Journal*, April 30, 2009, p. A13. Copyright © 2009 Dow Jones & Company, Inc. All rights reserved. Reprinted with permission of The *Wall Street Journal*.

3. Why does Haqqani say that the United States has been reluctant to share military equipment with Pakistan?

The specter of extremist Taliban taking over a nuclear-armed Pakistan is not only a gross exaggeration, it could also lead to misguided policy prescriptions from Pakistan's allies, including our friends in Washington [D.C.].

Pakistan Can Defeat the Taliban

Pakistan and the international community do face serious challenges in confronting terrorists and the ideologies that sustain them. But panicked reactions of the type witnessed in the U.S. media over the last few weeks [April 2009]—after the Taliban drove into Buner, a town 60 miles north of the capital Islamabad—are not conducive to strengthening Pakistani democracy or to developing an effective counterterrorism policy for Pakistan.

Now that the Taliban have been driven out of Buner, and Pakistani forces have militarily engaged them just outside their Swat Valley stronghold, it should be clear to all that Pakistan can and will defeat the Taliban.

In the free elections that returned Pakistan to democracy in February 2008, Pakistanis overwhelmingly rejected Taliban sympathizers and advocates of extremist Islamist ideologies. But the legacy of dictatorship, including a tolerance for some militant groups, has proven tough to erase. Anti-American rhetoric and Pakistan's traditional security concerns about its neighbors have also dampened popular enthusiasm for strong military action against violent extremists, even though President Asif Zardari has repeatedly declared the war against them a war for Pakistan's soul.

Meanwhile, the change of administration in the U.S. [with the election of Barack Obama in November 2008] has slowed the flow of assistance to Pakistan. Unfortunately, ordinary Pakistanis have begun to wonder if our alliance with the West is bringing any benefits at all.

Fighting the Taliban in Buner

The Pakistani government has launched a military operation in the Taliban-controlled district of Buner. The operation is the second in three days in the Malakand Division, a region recently ceded to the Taliban in a controversial peace agreement. . . .

Paramilitary fighters from the Frontier Corps backed by regular Army units, artillery, helicopter gunships, and attack aircraft moved into Buner this afternoon [April 2009] after the government warned the Taliban to "leave Buner or face action."

"The aim of the offensive is to eliminate and expel militants from Buner," Major General Athar Abbas, the Director-General of the Inter-Services Public Relations, said.

Bill Roggio, "Pakistan Launches Operation Against the Taliban in Buner," Long War Journal, April 28, 2009.
www.longwarjournal.com.

Under the [Pervez] Musharraf dictatorship [from 2001 to 2008], Pakistan probably was not as quick as it needed to be to comprehend the enormity of the Taliban threat. And after last year's election of democratic leaders, our new government had an array of domestic issues to address. Mobilizing all elements of national power, particularly public opinion, against the Taliban threat took time because many Pakistanis thought the Taliban were amenable to negotiations and would keep their word.

Recent developments offer us an opportunity amid crisis. More Pakistanis are now convinced of the need to confront the extremists.

Pakistan Can Become a Model

The recent spike of international concern about the threat in Pakistan seems to stem from the recent dialogue between the government of the Pashtunkhwa Northwest Frontier Province of Pakistan [a region also known as the Swat Valley] and a local movement that supported Islamic law but did not join the Taliban's violent campaign. The goal for this dialogue was twofold—first, to restore order and stability to the Swat Valley; and second, to wedge rational elements of the religiously conservative population away from terrorists and fanatics.

The model here was the successful pacification of Fallujah in Iraq [in 2007], where agreements with more moderate elements broke them away from al Qaeda [a terrorist group] nihilists. The model worked so well in Fallujah that it is now being resurrected by the American and NATO [North Atlantic Treaty Organization] troops in Afghanistan. The goal in Pakistan's Swat Valley was the same.

The dialogue in Swat resulted in an agreement that would allow for elements of Shariah [Islamic law] to be applied to the judicial system of the Valley, as it has at other times in our nation's history. This agreement demanded that the native Taliban put down their weapons, pledge nonviolence, and accept the writ of the state. It was a local solution for what some in Pakistan viewed as a local problem.

Let me be perfectly clear here: Pakistan's civil and military leadership understands that al Qaeda and its allies are not potential negotiating partners. But, as the U.S. did in Iraq, Pakistan sought to distinguish between reconcilable and irreconcilable elements within an expanding insurgency.

The premise of the dialogue was peace. Without peace there is no agreement, and without an agreement the Pakistani government will use all power at its disposal to restore order in the Valley. We'd rather negotiate than fight. But if we have to fight we will—and we will fight to win.

What does Pakistan need to contain this threat? In the short term we need the U.S. to share modern technology in antiterrorist engagement. Pakistan needs night-vision equipment, jammers that can knock out FM radio transmissions by the terrorists, and a larger, modernized fleet of helicopter gunships for ground support in the massive sweeps that are necessary to contain, repel and destroy the enemy.

Yet Washington has been reluctant to share this modern equipment, and to train our military in antiterrorism techniques, because of concerns that these systems could be used against India [a nation with which Pakistan has a history of tension]. Such concerns are misplaced. Pakistanis understand that the primary threat to our homeland today is not from our neighbor to the east [that is, India] but from the Federally Administered Tribal Areas (FATA) on our border with Afghanistan. To meet this threat, we must be provided the means to fight the terrorists while we work on resuming our composite dialogue with India.

In the long term, Pakistan's security will be predicated on Pakistan's economic viability. That is the central thrust of the Kerry-Lugar legislation currently before Congress, which would establish a 10-year, multibillion dollar commitment to Pakistan's economic and social system. It is also manifest in the Regional Opportunity Zone legislation currently before Congress that would open U.S. markets to products manufactured in Afghanistan and Pakistan's FATA region. An economically prosperous Pakistan will be less susceptible to the ideology of international terrorism—and it will become a model to a billion Muslims across the world that Islam and modernity under democracy are not only compatible, but can thrive together.

> *"Unless the Obama administration can get Pakistan's army to stop supporting the Taliban with weapons and logistical support, the insurgency will continue to threaten the U.S.-supported Kabul government."*

Pakistan Aids the Taliban

Selig S. Harrison

Selig S. Harrison is director of the Asia Program at the Center for International Policy. In the following viewpoint, he argues that elements of Pakistan's military provide the Taliban with weapons and support. Harrison says the U.S. government should threaten to cut off military aid to Pakistan unless Pakistan agrees to cease aiding the Taliban. Harrison believes the Pakistani military is so dependent on U.S. aid that these threats would be effective.

As you read, consider the following questions:

1. Why does Harrison believe that applying pressure on the civilian government of Pakistan will have little effect on military aid to the Taliban?

2. According to the viewpoint, what are CSFs?

3. Since 2001, what improvements has Pakistan made in its armed capabilities, according to Harrison?

Unless the [Barack] Obama administration can get Pakistan's army to stop supporting the Taliban with weapons and logistical support, the insurgency will continue to threaten the U.S.-supported Kabul [the capital of Afghanistan] government—no matter how many more troops the U.S. sends to Afghanistan.

Cut Military Aid

Pakistan's army and its powerful intelligence agencies control the country's role in Afghanistan. The outcome of the power struggle between Pakistani President Asif Ali Zardari and his rival, Nawaz Sharif, will not affect this reality. The army lets the elected civilian government run domestic affairs and handle economic aid, but it gets unfettered control of foreign and security policy, including military aid.

So it would not be enough for the U.S. to push Pakistan's shaky civilian leadership on the Taliban issue, and it is not desirable to do so while it is preoccupied with terrorist violence at home. To get Pakistan's cooperation in Afghanistan, Washington will have to face down the army, threatening to cut off its largely unmonitored military aid. But the Obama administration has shied away from this reality in its newly announced Afghanistan policy, seeking instead to buy off Islamabad [the capital of Pakistan] with more economic aid.

Since 9/11 [the September 11, 2001, terrorist attacks on the United States], the United States has given Pakistan $11.5 billion in economic and military aid—$7.5 billion of it in the form of direct cash subsidies to the armed forces, known as "Coalition Support Funds" (CSFs), provided for the express purpose of fighting the Taliban and other jihadists. Suspicions that Islamabad has been playing a double game have steadily grown, but it was not until nine months ago that definitive evidence of its support for the Taliban surfaced.

In his new book, *The Inheritance,* *New York Times* correspondent David Sanger reveals that "several" key U.S. intelligence officials told him of National Security Agency telephone intercepts in which Pakistan's army chief of staff, Gen. Ashfaq Kayani, referred to a key Taliban warlord, Jalaluddin Haqqani, as a "strategic asset." According to Sanger, another Pakistani general, in a meeting with the visiting U.S. director of national intelligence, Mike McConnell, explained that "we must sustain contact with the Taliban and support them" to make sure that in the future, the Afghan government "is a government friendly to Pakistan."

In my own reporting, I found that then-President Pervez Musharraf [Pakistan President from 2001–2008] did just enough to keep U.S. aid flowing by providing occasional intelligence information on al-Qaeda activities along the border while at the same time permitting the Taliban leader, Mullah Mohammed Omar, to set up his operational headquarters in the Pakistan border city of Quetta.

The United States Should Use Its Leverage

U.S. officials argued that Pakistan would stop providing intelligence on al-Qaeda if the U.S. forced a showdown on the Taliban issue. But Islamabad is so dependent on multiple forms of U.S. and U.S.-arranged economic and military aid that Washington has enormous bargaining leverage—hitherto unused.

To make the Musharraf regime solvent after 9/11, the U.S. orchestrated an extension of its $13.5 billion in foreign debt. Today the Pakistan economy would collapse if these debts were called in. Much of the $4 billion in economic and military aid approved by Congress during the Musharraf years is already in Pakistan's hands and cannot be used as a bargaining chip. But the U.S. has leverage in the overblown CSF subsidies. A Government Accountability Office probe last year suggests widespread fraud in the program and makes clear

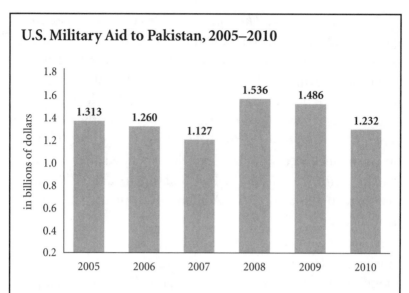

U.S. Military Aid to Pakistan, 2005–2010

TAKEN FROM: K. Alan Kronstadt, "Direct Overt U.S. Aid and Military Reimbursements to Pakistan, FY2002–FY2011," *Federation of American Scientists*, March 9, 2010. www.fas.org.

that it could be drastically cut without affecting what Pakistan does on the Afghan border.

Cuts would be painful

Threatening to cut CSF funds would get results because the money goes directly into the Pakistani treasury and—despite U.S. protests—makes it possible for Pakistan to beef up its military capabilities against India [Pakistan's neighbor, with which it has tense relations]. Since 2001, the army has doubled its heavy artillery, self-propelled howitzers and combat helicopters. It has also increased its armory of anti-tank missiles from 200 to 5,250. Faced with an end to these subsidies, the Pakistan army would become more cooperative on the Taliban issue.

Secretary of State Hillary Clinton used the threat of an economic aid cutoff [in March 2009] to get Zardari to compromise with Sharif and end the crisis in Islamabad [over the reinstatement of an important judge]. Now, military aid leverage should be used before resorting to the Predator missile strikes and commando raids on Taliban sanctuaries in populous Quetta that some U.S. officials are advocating.

A cutoff of Pakistani weapons and logistical support to the Taliban would make a major difference in the military struggle in Afghanistan.

Looking ahead, it would also make the Taliban more amenable to compromise in any future negotiations to end the war in Afghanistan that the Obama administration ultimately envisions.

| "In effect, Pakistan, a nuclear power, has relinquished its sovereignty over an important part of the country."

Pakistan Has Capitulated to the Taliban

Susanne Koelbl

Susanne Koelbl is a journalist whose work has appeared in the German newspaper der Spiegel. *In the following viewpoint, she reports on Pakistan's negotiated surrender of the Swat Valley to Taliban forces. She argues that the loss of the Swat Valley was caused in part by the fact that the Pakistani military is sympathetic to the Taliban, which it hopes will help counterbalance India's power in the long term. Koelbl concludes that Taliban control of the Swat Valley, with the imposition of strict Islamic law by arbitrary authorities, is disastrous for the people who live there.*

As you read, consider the following questions:

1. According to Koelbl, who used to visit the Swat Valley and for what purpose?
2. Who is Khalil Mullah, according to the viewpoint?

Susanne Koelbl, "Bowing Down to the Taliban," *Spiegel Online International,* February 21, 2009. Copyright © 9/2009 DER SPIEGEL. All rights reserved. Reproduced by permission.

3. What are some of the signs of Talibanization in Pakistan, according to Koelbl?

The defeat was celebrated as if it had been a victory. The chief minister of the North-West Frontier Province greeted a delegation from the local Taliban. The Taliban officials, with their long beards and turbans, had come to the chief minister's house to sign a treaty. After arriving in pickups and large limousines, the men were seated on velvet armchairs and served food on silver trays.

Then the pious foes of the government in Islamabad [the capital of Pakistan] were given a coveted piece of Pakistan as a gift.

Taliban Victory

Under the agreement, which the men and the governor signed with much ceremony, the Taliban will be permitted to implement their interpretation of Islamic law, or Sharia, in the Swat Valley and other adjacent districts at the foot of the Hindu Kush mountain range. "Today is a historic day," said Amir Haider Khan Hoti, the chief minister of the provincial government, clearly straining to put a positive spin on the Taliban's assumption of power. "An old demand of the people has been met. The new regulation will provide a more efficient legal system."

It was a blatant lie. Most Pakistanis are shocked by the prospect that, in the Swat Valley, thieves could have their hands cut off and adulterers could face stoning in the future. Such punishments were in fact already possible under Pakistani law, but have never been carried out in the past.

The Swat Valley in the Malakand region, with its sunny ski slopes and elegant resort hotels, was once one of Pakistan's biggest tourist attractions. The vast sky is almost always a clear blue, and the icy slopes seem close enough to touch. Swat, only about 250 kilometers (156 miles) north of the capital Islamabad, was a haven for wealthy city residents, who came here to enjoy the fresh, clean air or hike along mountain brooks and through apricot groves.

The valley's residents have little in common with the bigoted Taliban. Only last year, local citizens voted the Islamists out of office and gave the overwhelming majority of their votes to the semi-secular, liberal Awami National Party. But then they were again left with the Taliban, with the consent of the army and Pakistani President Asif Ali Zardari.

The news of the radical Islamists' takeover of the Swat Valley was just as alarming to the rest of the world as it was to many in Pakistan. Richard Holbrooke, the US's new special envoy for the region, was in India, having just left Pakistan after completing his first official visit to the country, when he received the "horrifying" news. According to Holbrooke, the Taliban victory shows that India, Pakistan and the United States face a common enemy "that poses direct threats to our leaderships, our capitals and our people." In the wake of its growing successes in putting pressure on American and NATO [North Atlantic Treaty Organization] troops in Afghanistan, the Taliban must now feel that repression and terror against ordinary people and army personnel in Pakistan will lead to further gains.

This week [February 2009], the chief of Pakistan's army, Ashfaq Parvez Kayani, and Pakistani Foreign Minister Shah Mehmood Qureshi are meeting with US officials in Washington as part of talks which will inform a review of US policy in Afghanistan, in which the situation in Pakistan plays a key role.

In Islamabad, President Zardari sought to downplay the defeat, noting that the agreement with the radicals requires them to lay down their weapons. But hardly anyone believes this. Even government officials in the affected region admit that "the Taliban are using the truce to rearm." Taliban militants announced Tuesday they had indefinitely extended the cease-fire in the Swat Valley which was due to expire on Wednesday, allowing more time for peace talks with the government. But a Mingora resident suspects that this is only in order to avoid their troops being disarmed.

In effect, Pakistan, a nuclear power, has relinquished its sovereignty over an important part of the country.

Terrorizing Civilians

The once-idyllic Swat Valley has been in a state of war since 2007. The military sent a total of 12,000 troops to the region in an attempt to curb the influence of the extremists, who have beheaded 70 policemen, banned girls' education and destroyed hundred of schools in the valley.

The clashes resulted in a great deal of bloodshed, including the deaths of at least 1,200 civilians and 180 Pakistani soldiers. But the outcome of these military operations was fatal for the government. Today, the Taliban control more than 80 percent of the Malakand region, compared with only a handful of villages a year ago [in 2008].

Civilians found themselves caught between the combatants. "The army ordered us to leave the village ahead of the fighting, but the Taliban forced us to stay there," a frantic hotel owner reports by telephone from a village near Malam Jabba, once a popular ski resort. Like the region's 10,000 other refugees, he has found temporary shelter with relatives, but plans to leave the area as soon as possible. According to the hotel owner, more and more Swat residents are submitting to the Taliban in an effort to survive.

Many even claim that the military has deliberately spared the Taliban leadership to avoid provoking further Taliban animosity against itself and the government. Others believe that the security forces were just too weak to defeat the 3,000 armed extremists. Both views are probably correct. The militants installed their regime in the mountainous tribal areas after being ousted from Afghanistan in 2001. Now their power is starting to spill over into Pakistan's heartland, which includes the Swat Valley.

After the sun has set in the Swat Valley, small groups of men furtively enter the house of Khalil Mullah. The visitors are Taliban spies, and they have come to report to Khalil— whose name means "friend" in Arabic—about who has broken the laws of Allah in the region they control. They will report who has been seen dancing exuberantly, had his beard shaved, committed adultery or expressed sympathy for the government in Islamabad—in short, who is a traitor.

Khalil Mullah begins his daily radio show on FM 91, a Taliban radio station, at about 8 p.m. The residents of the snow-covered plateau listen to Khalil's religious broadcast to hear the names he reads at the end. Acting as both judge and prosecutor, he announces the names of those required to appear before the Taliban's Sharia count—and of those who have already been sentenced.

The bodies of these unfortunate residents can be found the next morning on the market square in Mingora. The corpses are hanging by their legs, their heads cut off and placed onto the soles of their feet as a final form of disgrace for the dead. A note under each body reads: "The same penalty will await those who dare to remove or bury these spies and traitors."

The extremists are led by Maulana Fazlullah, 33, a self-proclaimed cleric who once worked as a laborer on a ski lift. The people of Malakand call him simply the "radio mullah." It was Fazlullah who first took his terrorist network to the airwaves.

In his broadcasts, he promised more efficiency and justice to citizens disappointed by the corrupt and lethargic Pakistani authorities. But the station quickly turned into a parallel government of sorts. In each day's broadcast, Fazlullah's holy warriors issue new rules that reflect their own interpretation of Sharia. Women are already banned from visiting markets, under penalty of death, and girls prohibited from attending school. Police officers who obey orders from Islamabad risk having their ears cut off or being killed. Some 800 policemen have already deserted their posts to join the Taliban.

The death lists draw no class distinctions and include people from all walks of life. The Taliban's victims range from barbers and teachers to tribal elders, ministers and more liberal clerics who oppose Fazlullah.

Supporting the Taliban

Politicians in Islamabad had long deluded themselves over how much power the Pakistani Taliban had already attained. In a recent interview with the American CBS television network, Zardari admitted that he had been misled about the scope of the problems in the north. "Everybody was in denial that they're weak and they won't be able to take over—that they won't be able to give us a challenge," he told the station.

Zardari's bitter realization is consistent with the picture that Mike McConnell, the former director of the US National Security Agency (NSA), formed when he visited Pakistan. He met several times with the military leadership in Islamabad last year. During one of these meetings, a Pakistani two-star general told him why the army, which has always been the dominant political power in Pakistan, complies with the politicians' demands to fight the Taliban while at the same time secretly supporting the group.

The officers do not expect the United States to remain in Afghanistan in the long term. They fear that India [Pakistan's neighbor, and a country with which it has had longstanding tensions] will advance into the power vacuum that will be left behind when American troops withdraw. For this reason, the Pakistanis are unwilling to give up their ties to the Afghan opposition, the Taliban. In a recently published book on the foreign policy challenges President Barack Obama has inherited,

New York Times author David Sanger quotes the Pakistani two-star general as saying: "We must support the Taliban."

Pakistan's military remains more concerned about a conflict with India than about Islamist terror at home. As a result, it accepts Talibanization as a necessary evil, allowing, for example, such changes as women no longer being accepted as customers in restaurants or tailors' shops—even in Lahore, a liberal major city home to many intellectuals. "The influence of the extremists is being ignored and it's spreading like a virus," observes Gregor Enste, director of the Heinrich Boell Foundation in Lahore.

Despite the imposition of Sharia law, many citizens of the Swat Valley town of Mingora celebrated in the streets and gave each other gifts of sweets. After the bloodshed of recent months, they were pleased to see peace restored to the region, under almost any circumstances.

The Taliban's chief negotiator, 77-year-old Islamist Sufi Mohammed, is the father-in-law of Maulana Fazlullah, Swat's brutal new ruler. Sufi Mohammed has now begun traveling through the villages with his so-called peace caravan to celebrate the triumph of Sharia over secular law. The government in Islamabad hopes that the somewhat more restrained father-in-law will exert a moderating influence on the power-hungry Fazlullah.

But there is little reason to be too hopeful. Like all Islamists, Sufi Mohammed is also an unbending enemy of democracy, which he has always seen as a system "that was forced upon us by the infidels." During his tour through the Swat Valley, he explains again and again: "True Islam permits neither elections nor democracy."

"Pakistani officials have taken a sudden interest in promoting peace in Afghanistan, a change analysts attribute to a combination of self-interest and fear."

Pakistan Seeks Role as Mediator in Possible Taliban-Afghanistan Peace Talks

Pamela Constable

Pamela Constable is a Washington Post *staff writer who has covered South Asia and Afghanistan. In the following viewpoint, she reports that Pakistan has become interested in trying to mediate between the Taliban and the Afghan government. She says that Pakistan has long-standing links to the Taliban that may be helpful in brokering peace, though such links also could backfire. Constable concludes that Pakistan is motivated by concerns about Indian influence in Afghanistan and by fear that the war in Afghanistan may worsen its own problems with Muslim extremists.*

Pamela Constable, "Pakistan Seeks Role as Mediator in Possible Taliban-Afghanistan Peace Talks," *Washington Post*, January 28, 2010. Copyright © 2010 The Washington Post. Reprinted with permission.

As you read, consider the following questions:

1. What are some reasons analysts give as to why an overt mediation role by the Pakistani government with the Taliban could backfire?
2. Who is Mohammed Omar?
3. What have the U.S. and the Afghan governments promised rank-and-file Taliban members to wean them away from the Taliban, according to Constable?

L ahore, Pakistan—Pakistan, which once sponsored Taliban forces but turned against them under American pressure in 2001, now hopes to play a role as a broker in proposed negotiations among Taliban leaders and the Afghan government, with support from the United States.

As leaders of 60 countries meet in London on Thursday to discuss how to help Afghanistan stop its downward spiral into instability, the possibilities for reconciliation and talks with both Taliban leaders and foot soldiers will top the agenda.

Until recently, Pakistan had been on hostile terms with the neighboring government in Kabul and had sought to distance itself from the problems of insurgency across the border, while struggling to curb a homegrown Taliban movement that has carried out dozens of bombings and suicide attacks in Pakistan in the past several years.

Now, however, Pakistani officials have taken a sudden interest in promoting peace in Afghanistan, a change analysts attribute to a combination of self-interest and fear. Pakistan, they say, hopes a power-sharing arrangement in Kabul that includes the Taliban would be friendlier to its interests; and it worries that if the Afghan conflict drags on, its domestic extremist problem will spin out of control.

But analysts said any overt mediation role by the Pakistani government could backfire for several reasons, including deep mistrust among Afghan leaders, unpredictable reactions by

Pakistani militants, Taliban resentment of pressure from its former backers and unrealistic Pakistani expectations of Western gratitude.

"The crisis in Pakistan has created a big change in its thinking. The country is suffering enormously from the Pakistani Taliban, and this may be a way to get off the hook," said Ahmed Rashid, a Lahore-based expert on the Taliban and on Afghanistan-Pakistan relations. "Pakistan still exerts some influence on the Afghan Taliban, but Kabul will be extremely wary of Pakistani bias. It is a very tricky situation."

U.S. officials are watching the evolution of Pakistani thinking with interest.

"What this is really about is whether the Pakistanis want to be part of the problem or part of the solution," said one American diplomat who spoke on the condition of anonymity.

Pakistani President Asif Ali Zardari, who met with Afghan President Hamid Karzai in Turkey this week, said there is an urgent need for peace talks. Echoing Karzai's comments about the Taliban being "sons of the soil," Zardari said that if insurgents are "reconcilable and want to give up their way of life, a democracy always welcomes them back."

The Real Key Players

The key Pakistani players in this drama are not civilian leaders but the army and especially the Inter-Services Intelligence agency (ISI), which once sponsored the Taliban, worked closely with the group when it ruled Afghanistan in the late 1990s and reportedly has continued to assist Taliban leaders in exile after the regime was overthrown by U.S.-backed Afghan forces in 2001.

Rashid said the Afghan militants have been chafing under the Pakistani agency's efforts to control them. Other analysts said Pakistan's influence on the Taliban waned years ago, when the militia's leaders ignored Islamabad's pleas to spare the historic Bamiyan Buddha statues and to turn over al-Qaeda leader Osama bin Laden to the Americans.

But the analysts also said that with so many Taliban leaders and their families based in Pakistan, their relations with that nation are still close—perhaps too close for officials in Kabul, who have seen their fledgling postwar democracy torn apart by renewed conflict and hundreds of terrorist attacks in the past several years.

In a newspaper interview with McClatchy published this week, a former Pakistani intelligence official described the Taliban as "big-hearted" and extremely loyal to Mohammed Omar, the movement's fugitive leader. He called Omar a reasonable, patriotic man who has no desire to ruin his country. "He's the only answer," the officer said.

Omar has vehemently rejected any suggestion of talks, and experts said the Taliban forces, which are now active in 33 of Afghanistan's 34 provinces, feel confident they can outlast the international military presence. Some analysts who favor talks said they doubt rank-and-file Taliban members could be weaned away from the cause with promises of jobs and money, a pillar of the U.S. and Afghan reintegration proposal.

Other Afghan insurgent leaders have hinted at a more open outlook. A close aide to Gulbuddin Hekmatyar, a fugitive former militia leader who now opposes the West, told a meeting in the Pakistani city of Peshawar this week that Pakistan can "play a major role" and even achieve a "breakthrough" by brokering an Afghan peace process.

A Unique Relationship

Several military experts said that although Pakistan's longtime relationship with the Taliban has put it in a unique position to promote negotiations, it could also undermine them. They said the country must prove to Afghanistan and the world that after years of trying to manipulate Afghan politics, it now wants to take a constructive and neutral stance.

"Pakistan needs to reassure Karzai and the Americans that it wants to play a very different role this time," said Talat Masood, a retired Pakistani general and analyst in Islamabad, the capital. "The Taliban should welcome Pakistan as an interlocutor if they are willing to compromise, but if the ISI overplays its hand, it could upset a very delicate situation."

Officials at the Pakistani foreign ministry could not be reached for comment on the issue this week, nor could army spokesmen. But some analysts said that by offering to help resolve the Afghan conflict, Pakistani officials are hoping chiefly to bolster the country's stature and security—possibly at the expense of its next-door rival India, which has established a robust presence in Afghanistan.

"Pakistan's role could be crucial, but it will not do this for free. It will only facilitate these talks to protect its national interests," Rashid said. "It will demand its pound of flesh."

> *"Pakistan's approach to the Taliban amounts to appeasement. The United States should not abet this strategy."*

Pakistan Has Done a Poor Job Negotiating with the Taliban

Sharad Joshi

Sharad Joshi is a postdoctoral fellow at the James Martin Center for Nonproliferation Studies in Monterey, California. In the following viewpoint, he argues that Pakistan's negotiations with the Taliban have emboldened the militants without making peace any more likely. He notes that the agreements with the Taliban do not require them to disarm or to cease launching attacks into Afghanistan. Joshi argues that negotiation with some elements of the Taliban eventually will be necessary, but argues that such agreements should make continued violence less, rather than more, likely.

As you read, consider the following questions:

1. Who is Baitullah Mehsud?

2. According to Joshi, what have Pakistani authorities refused to acknowledge about al Qaeda?

Sharad Joshi, "Is Pakistan Appeasing the Taliban?" *Foreign Policy in Focus*, June 13, 2008. Copyright © 2008 Institute for Policy Studies. Reproduced by permission.

3. Under what circumstances were ten Pakistani soldiers killed by U.S. airstrikes, according to Joshi?

In May 2008, in the midst of the ongoing Taliban insurgency in Afghanistan, Islamabad [that is, Pakistan's capital] concluded at least two peace agreements with Taliban and Taliban-linked groups operating in Pakistan. Although negotiations with the Taliban are necessary for any broad-based peace settlement in the region, these agreements threaten to complicate policy options for Washington [D.C.] and the Hamid Karzai government in Afghanistan.

Concessions offered to the Taliban can potentially strengthen its capabilities and bases in the Federally Administered Tribal Areas, which borders Afghanistan and contains the volatile North and South Waziristan provinces. From these bases, Taliban militants have a history of infiltrating and launching cross-border attacks into Afghanistan.

Pakistan's approach to the Taliban amounts to appeasement.[1] The United States should not abet this strategy by taking off the table such sticks as cross-border raids on Taliban bases.

The Agreements Between Pakistan and the Taliban

The basic objective of the agreements is to end terrorist strikes and insurgent violence in Pakistan, which experienced a dramatic upsurge in 2007. The first deal was with the main Taliban group operating in Pakistan, the Tehrik-i-Taliban Pakistan, or the Pakistani Taliban, which is led by Baitullah Mehsud, a suspect in the assassination of former prime minister Benazir Bhutto [killed prior to national elections in 2008]. The Pakistani Taliban, based in Waziristan in the Federally Administered Tribal Areas (FATA) is committed to stopping insurgent and terrorist attacks.

1. A policy of making concessions to avoid war, associated with Britain's widely condemned policy toward Adolf Hitler before World War II.

In return, Pakistan has withdrawn its forces from territory controlled by the Pakistani Taliban, left camps and weapons with the Taliban, and halted all military operations against them. At the same time regarding Afghanistan, Islamabad had denied responsibility for dealing with cross-border violence, saying that the Kabul [the capital of Afghanistan] government will have to handle this problem. Thus, in return for stopping attacks, Taliban control over the tribal areas (FATA) is strengthened further.

As part of the agreement, Pakistan also released two senior Taliban commanders from Afghanistan—Mullah Obaidullah Akhund (deputy to Taliban leader Mullah Omar) and Mullah Mansoor Dadullah—along with hundreds of other militants in exchange for over 30 army soldiers and officers as well as the Pakistani ambassador to Afghanistan who had been captured by the Taliban in early 2008. The agreement does not oblige the Pakistani Taliban to disarm and in fact releases hundreds of militants who can potentially take up arms again, in Pakistan as well as in Afghanistan. There is also no indication that training camps for suicide bombers run by Mehsud's group in Waziristan will be shut down. Moreover, parallel to the negotiations, the Pakistan army also slowed down its operations against insurgents.

In a second agreement, Islamabad and the government of the North West Frontier Province (NWFP), which borders Afghanistan, made peace with the Tehrik-e-Nifaz-e-Shariat-e-Mohammadi (TNSM) which had fought the military in the Swat Valley district of the province. Again, several militant leaders and hundreds of militants have been released. The Pakistan military will also withdraw from the Taliban-infested Swat Valley, and in return militants will end their campaign against the Pakistani army. Although this area does not directly border Afghanistan, concessions to militant outfits without any meaningful, permanent obligations on the part of these groups does not bode well for a comprehensive peace settlement that involves the broader Taliban umbrella group, including the group's leadership in Afghanistan. According to recent reports, Islamabad is scrapping the Swat agreement due to continued suicide attacks. Nevertheless, Islamabad is still willing to deal with militant groups without pressuring them to roll back their armed capability, which then ensures further terrorist incidents.

Appeasement Will Not Bring Peace

Islamabad's argument for such a narrow and Pakistan-centric agreement is that it can no longer bear the violent consequences of the U.S.-led war on terror. But although it is essential that militant groups be brought into the dialogue process, the absence of any significant and permanent rollback of their terror infrastructure dooms the long-term prospects of such agreements, Islamabad's argument also fails to consider that although the U.S.-led campaign against terror has given a fillip to militant outfits, there already was a decades-old militant infrastructure in Pakistan that merely reactivated itself in the form of the Pakistani Taliban in a violent, insular manner.

Finally, these negotiations ignore the presence of the Afghan Taliban in Pakistan, whose leadership, including Taliban supreme leader Mullah Omar, is widely suspected to be based in the Baluchistan capital of Quetta. In general, these deals still leave militant groups in positions of strength and without any qualitative decrease in their capabilities. As the attack on the Danish embassy in Islamabad in early June [2008] showed, there is no indication that al-Qaeda will halt its terrorist attacks. It claimed responsibility for the attack and continues to help train Taliban militants in the border areas. Furthermore, the agreement does not focus adequately on the removal of foreign militants who are based in the tribal areas and part of the al-Qaeda network there. Pakistani authorities have in fact refused to acknowledge that Al Qaeda actually does maintain camps in the tribal areas.

Afghan Security Forces

President [Barack] Obama and his advisers have decided to significantly expand Afghanistan's security forces....

A plan awaiting final approval ... would set a goal of about 400,000 troops and national police officers, more than twice the forces' current size, and more than three times the size that American officials believed would be adequate for Afghanistan in 2002.

Thom Shanker and Eric Schmitt,
"U.S. Plans Vastly Expanded Afghan Security Force,"
New York Times, *March 18, 2009. www.nytimes.com.*

In 2006 Islamabad concluded a previous deal with militants in Waziristan, including Mehsud. That initiative is widely regarded as a failure because the Pakistani army evacuated these areas and militant groups were able to eventually regroup and step up violence in Pakistan and Afghanistan. It is not clear to what extent the Pakistani Taliban will stick to the latest agreement in Pakistan, given that its commander, Mehsud, has demanded that Pakistan end its alliance with the United States as a condition for the deal to hold.

Options for Afghan and U.S.-Led Forces

NATO [North Atlantic Treaty Organization] and Afghan forces fear that the agreement will reduce pressure on the Taliban in the border tribal areas of Pakistan, allow it to consolidate their bases and training camps, and increase attacks across the border. Not required to disarm, the Taliban will essentially remain in control of the areas under their occupation. Moreover, as already mentioned, Islamabad has made it clear that its objective is to stop violence in Pakistan and that they are not responsible for what happens in Afghanistan. Taliban leaders, especially Baitullah Mehsud, the head of the Pakistani Taliban, have said that they would continue attacking Afghan and multinational forces across the border.

Thus, current and future NATO/Afghan policy options will have to factor in the consequences of the Islamabad-Taliban deal. As it happens, in the last year, [2008] NATO/ Afghan forces have been battling an increasingly assertive Taliban that has occupied parts of southern Afghanistan and has been bolstered by increased drug profits. Attacks in Afghanistan originating from Pakistan have doubled in recent months compared to last year and have especially involved non-Afghan militants.

These latest agreements call into question Washington's proposals to fund and train the Frontier Corps, a paramilitary outfit under the Pakistani ministry of interior. Although the Pakistani military is supposed to move out of the south Waziristan area, the Frontier Corps will be allowed into these areas. However, despite $50 million in U.S. funds in 2007 for training and equipment supply, this force is badly trained and not suitable for fighting militants, as previous encounters have demonstrated. This plan is also complicated by the suspicion among U.S. agencies that the Frontier Corps has actually been assisting Taliban militants in the tribal areas, as opposed to combating them.

Apart from the Taliban, another re-emerging opposition force in Afghanistan is the Hezb-i-Islami, led by Gulbuddin Hekmatyar, a prominent Mujahideen [the name for the Muslim opposition to the Soviet Union] leader during the anti-Soviet campaign in the 1980s and closely connected to the Pakistani establishment, especially before the rise of the Taliban in 1994. Recent attacks in Afghanistan have hinted at a growing alliance between Hezb-i-Islami and the Taliban. Hekmatyar's influence among government officials is significant and provides avenues and information to aid attacks.

The Karzai government has offered talks and also considered inviting the Taliban and Hezb-i-Islami to join the government to provide some stability. There have reportedly been some overtures by the Taliban. However, the Taliban's objectives, which include the departure of multinational forces and possibly the eventual takeover of Afghanistan, would be too high a price, and certainly unacceptable to the U.S.-led force. While moderate elements of the Taliban do need to be co-opted into the political process the question is what concessions would they want in return and whether they would permanently give up violence as a strategy. NATO allies operating in Afghanistan, including the United States, have also considered opening up lines of communication with moderate elements of the Taliban. But such dialogue must be part of a more comprehensive process that reinforces the primacy of the Kabul government. The strategy here should be to push back Taliban forces and then negotiate with relatively moderate elements from a strong position. Perhaps an Afghan version of a "surge" could be considered, if troop levels could be raised in the short-term, but that is unlikely.

A key long-term requirement for Afghanistan is increasing the capacity of the national government in Kabul to impose its authority and take the lead in counter-insurgency operations as well as rolling back drug production. This requires a broad-based approach including a credible alternative to poppy production [poppies are used to make the narcotic opium] for the farmers. At the same time, governance problems, especially corruption, also have to be addressed. However, in the absence of some degree of stability and decrease in violence, it is difficult to implement such measures effectively. The need to maintain de jure control of some provinces forces unpleasant compromises with warlords in Afghanistan who might have their own private agendas, whether skimming off government funds or engaging in the drug trade. The Karzai government has to wean itself from dependence on warlords and instead encourage the growth of legitimate political parties, which might provide an alternative mechanism for opposition militants through which to enter the political mainstream.

More Troops, Firmer Negotiations

Uncertainty also governs policy options available to Kabul and the U.S.-led multinational forces. According to outgoing NATO commander in Afghanistan, Gen. Dan McNeill, thousands more troops are needed. Increasing multinational troop levels in the short-term is unlikely to take place despite recent debates over increasing foreign troops. The Afghan National Army (ANA) is the obvious entity to take the lead in combating the Taliban, and its strength has risen to about 75,000 following training by NATO forces. However, this is less than half the number of troops required. Moreover, another key force, the Afghan police, is even further behind in terms of training.

Finally, in their talks with their Pakistani interlocutors, U.S. officials have broached the possibility of conducting cross-border raids on Taliban bases in Pakistan, but Islamabad has dismissed this proposal outright. Apart from the obvious problems arising from violation of Pakistani sovereignty, it would also lead to an even greater increase in anti-American sentiment in Pakistan. But in the absence of further multinational troops, the United States might be forced to resort to more intensified missile attacks on the Pakistani side of the border if there is an increase in the levels of attacks across the border following the agreement.

Thus, in the most recent incident, on June 10, [2008] U.S. forces carried out an air strike on Taliban militants on the Pakistan side of the border who had clashed with Afghan forces. At least 10 Pakistani troops who were supporting the militants were killed in the attack. Such incidents show that concessions that embolden the Taliban will inevitably lead to an escalation of violence both on the Pakistan side of the border as well as in Afghanistan.

Pakistan's policy of initiating a dialogue with the Taliban is important for peace and stability. However, such a negotiating strategy has to be a "carrot and stick" policy. In this case, the proverbial "stick" is being thrown away by Islamabad making this policy little different from appeasement. In the current initiative, the concessions offered by Islamabad ensure that the Taliban can regroup in the border areas to increase attacks not just in Afghanistan, but also in Pakistan, if needed.

Militant activity in Pakistan is a transnational phenomena. All affected parties, including those from Afghanistan, have to be included in the process. Simultaneously, there has to be a political dialogue process within Afghanistan as well, involving the Taliban and the Hezb-i-Islami, albeit without the kind of concessions made by Islamabad. Ideally, this would be coupled with a strengthened Afghan military with an assertive strategy rather than a reactive one. In the short-term however, with this agreement the Taliban has gained the upper hand in the Pakistani tribal areas and now looks westward across the Durand Line [the border between Pakistan and Afghanistan].

> *"Some two million people [in Cambodia] are believed to have died from executions, starvation, and forced labor in the camps established by . . . the Khmer Rouge. . . . Could the same thing happen in Pakistan today?"*

The U.S. War May Allow the Taliban to Seize Control of Pakistan

Pratap Chatterjee

Pratap Chatterjee is an Indian/Sri Lankan investigative journalist and author of Iraq, Inc.: A Profitable Occupation. *In the following viewpoint, he argues that American air strikes against militants in Pakistan are similar to American air strikes against militants in Cambodia in 1969. The Cambodian airstrikes helped to undermine the government, allowing radical groups to take over and murder a quarter of Cambodia's population. Chatterjee warns that drone strikes into Pakistan could destabilize that government. This, he concludes, could allow the Taliban to take over, and might create the conditions for a tragedy similar to the one that occurred in Cambodia.*

Pratap Chatterjee, "Operation Breakfast Redux," TOMDISPATCH.com, February 8, 2010. Reproduced by permission of the author.

As you read, consider the following questions:

1. What was Operation Breakfast?
2. Who was Norodom Sihanouk?
3. According to this viewpoint, 35 percent of Pakistanis disapprove of U.S. airstrikes into Pakistan even under what circumstances?

Sitting in air-conditioned comfort, cans of Coke and 7-Up within reach as they watched their screens, the ground controllers gave the order to strike under the cover of darkness. There had been no declaration of war. No advance warning, nothing, in fact, that would have alerted the "enemy" to the sudden, unprecedented bombing raids. The secret computer-guided strikes were authorized by the chairman of the Joint Chiefs of Staff, just weeks after a new American president entered the Oval Office. They represented an effort to wipe out the enemy's central headquarters whose location intelligence experts claimed to have pinpointed just across the border from the war-torn land where tens of thousands of American troops were fighting daily.

In remote villages where no reporters dared to go, far from the battlefields where Americans were dying, who knew whether the bombs that rained from the night sky had killed high-level insurgents or innocent civilians? For 14 months the raids continued and, after each one was completed, the commander of the bombing crews was instructed to relay a one-sentence message: "The ball game is over."

Operation Breakfast

The campaign was called "Operation Breakfast," and, while it may sound like the [Central Intelligence Agency] CIA's present [2010] air campaign over Pakistan, it wasn't. You need to turn the clock back to another American war, four decades earlier, to March 18, 1969, to be exact. The target was an area of Cambodia known as the Fish Hook that jutted into South

Vietnam, and Operation Breakfast would be but the first of dozens of top secret bombing raids. Later ones were named "Lunch," "Snack," and "Supper," and they went under the collective label "Menu." They were authorized by President Richard Nixon and were meant to destroy a (nonexistent) "Bamboo Pentagon," a central headquarters in the Cambodian borderlands where North Vietnamese communists were supposedly orchestrating raids deep into South Vietnam.

Like President [Barack] Obama today, Nixon had come to power promising stability in an age of unrest and with a vague plan to bringing peace to a nation at war. On the day he was sworn in, he read from the Biblical book of Isaiah: "They shall beat their swords into plowshares, and their spears into pruning hooks." He also spoke of transforming Washington's bitter partisan politics into a new age of unity: "We cannot learn from one another until we stop shouting at one another, until we speak quietly enough so that our words can be heard as well as our voices."

In recent years, many commentators and pundits have resorted to "the Vietnam analogy," comparing first the American war in Iraq and now in Afghanistan to the Vietnam War. Despite a number of similarities, the analogy disintegrates quickly enough if you consider that U.S. military campaigns in postinvasion Afghanistan and Iraq against small forces of lightly-armed insurgents bear little resemblance to the large-scale war that Presidents Lyndon B. Johnson and Richard Nixon waged against both southern revolutionary guerrillas and the military of North Vietnamese leader Ho Chi Minh, who commanded a real army, with the backing of, and supplies from, the Soviet Union and China.

A more provocative—and perhaps more ominous—analogy today might be between the CIA's escalating drone war in the contemporary Pakistani tribal borderlands and Richard Nixon's secret bombing campaign against the Cambodian equivalent. To briefly-recapitulate that ancient history: In the late 1960s, Cambodia was ruled by a "neutralist" king, Norodom Sihanouk, leading a weak government that had little relevance to its poor and barely educated citizens. In its borderlands, largely beyond its control, the North Vietnamese and Vietcong found "sanctuaries."

Sihanouk, helpless to do anything, looked the other way. In the meantime, sheltered by local villagers in distant areas of rural Cambodia was a small insurgent group, little-known communist fundamentalists who called themselves the Khmer Rouge. (Think of them as the 1970s equivalent of the Pakistani Taliban who have settled into the wild borderlands of that country largely beyond the control of the Pakistani government.) They were then weak and incapable of challenging Sihanouk—until, that is, those secret bombing raids by American B-52s began. As these intensified in the summer of 1969, areas of the country began to destabilize (helped on in 1970 by a U.S.-encouraged military coup in the capital Phnom Penh), and the Khmer Rouge began to gain strength.

You know the grim end of that old story.

Pakistan May End Like Cambodia

Forty years, almost to the day, after Operation Breakfast began, I traveled to the town of Snuol, close to where the American bombs once fell. It is a quiet town, no longer remote, as modern roads and Chinese-led timber companies have systematically cut down the jungle that once sheltered antigovernment rebels. I went in search of anyone who remembered the bombing raids, only to discover that few there were old enough to have been alive at the time, largely because the Khmer Rouge executed as much as a quarter of the total Cambodian population after they took power in 1975.

Eventually, a 15-minute ride out of town, I found an old soldier living by himself in a simple one-room house adorned with pictures of the old king, Sihanouk. His name was Kong Kan and he had first moved to the nearby town of Memot in

1960. A little further away, I ran into three more old men, Choenung Klou, Keo Long, and Hoe Huy, who had gathered at a newly built temple to chat.

All of them remembered the massive 1969 B-52 raids vividly and the arrival of U.S. troops the following year. "We thought the Americans had come to help us," said Choenung Klou. "But then they left and the [South] Vietnamese soldiers who came with them destroyed the villages and raped the women."

He had no love for the North Vietnamese communists either. "They would stay at people's houses, take our hammocks and food. We didn't like them and we were afraid of them."

Caught between two Vietnamese armies and with American planes carpet-bombing the countryside, increasing numbers of Cambodians soon came to believe that the Khmer Rouge, who were their countrymen, might help them. Like the Taliban of today, many of the Khmer Rouge were, in fact, teenage villagers who had responded, under the pressure of war and disruption, to the distant call of an inspirational ideology and joined the resistance in the jungles.

"If you ask me why I joined the Khmer Rouge, the main reason is because of the American invasion," Hun Sen, the current prime minister of Cambodia, has said. "If there was no invasion, by now, I would be a pilot or a professor."

Six years after the bombings of Cambodia began, shortly after the last helicopter lifted off the U.S. embassy in Saigon and the flow of military aid to the crumbling government of Cambodia stopped, a reign of terror took hold in the capital, Phnom Penh.

The Khmer Rouge left the jungles and entered the capital where they began a systemic genocide against city dwellers and anyone who was educated. They vowed to restart history at Year Zero, a new era in which much of the past became irrelevant. Some two million people are believed to have died from executions, starvation, and forced labor in the camps established by the Angkar leadership of the Khmer Rouge commanded by Pol Pot.

Could the same thing happen in Pakistan today? A new American president [Barack Obama] was ordering escalating drone attacks, in a country where no war has been declared, at the moment when I flew from Cambodia across South Asia to Afghanistan, so this question loomed large in my mind. Both there and just across the border, Operation Breakfast seems to be repeating itself.

In the Afghan capital, Kabul, I met earnest aid workers who drank late into the night in places like L'Atmosphere, a foreigner-only bar that could easily have doubled as a movie set for Saigon in the 1960s. Like modern-day equivalents of Graham Greene's "quiet American,"[1] these "consultants" describe a Third Way that is neither Western nor fundamentalist Islam.

At the very same time, CIA analysts in distant Virginia are using pilot-less drones and satellite technology to order strikes against supposed terrorist headquarters across the border in Pakistan. They are not so unlike the military men who watched radar screens in South Vietnam in the 1960s as the Cambodian air raids went on.

More Drone Attacks

In 2009, on the orders of President Obama, the U.S. unloaded more missiles and bombs on Pakistan than President [George W.] Bush did in the years of his secret drone war, and the strikes have been accelerating in number and intensity. By this January [2010], there was a drone attack almost every other day. Even if, this time around, no one is using the code phrase, "the ball game is over," Washington continually hails success after success, terrorist leader after terrorist leader killed,

1. Graham Greene was a British novelist; his book, *The Quiet American*, published in 1955, focused on western intervention in Vietnam.

Pakistani Opinion of U.S. Air Strikes, 2009

Missile strikes...	Agree %	Disagree %	Don't know %
Are necessary	34	58	8
Kill too many civilians	93	5	2
Are conducted without Pakistani government approval	58	27	14

The figures represent the opinions of the 32% of Pakistanis who were aware of the air strikes.

TAKEN FROM: Pew Global Attitudes Project, "Pakistani Public Opinion," August 13, 2009. http://pewglobal.org.

implying that something approaching victory could be somewhere just over the horizon.

As in the 1960s in Cambodia, these strikes are, in actuality, having a devastating, destabilizing effect in Pakistan, not just on the targeted communities, but on public consciousness throughout the region. An article in the Jan. 23 [2010] *New York Times* indicated that the fury over these attacks has even spread into Pakistan's military establishment which, in a manner similar to Sihanouk in the 1960s, knows its limits in its tribal borderlands and is publicly uneasy about U.S. air strikes which undermine the country's sovereignty. "Are you with us or against us?" the newspaper quoted a senior Pakistani military officer demanding of Secretary of Defense Robert Gates when he spoke last month at Pakistan's National Defense University.

Even pro-American Prime Minister Yousuf Raza Gilani has spoken out publicly against drone strikes. Of one such attack, he recently told reporters, "We strongly condemn this attack and the government will raise this issue at [the] diplomatic level."

Despite the public displays of outrage, however, the American strikes have undoubtedly been tacitly approved at the highest levels of the Pakistani government because of that country's inability to control militants in its tribal borderlands. Similarly, Sihanouk finally looked the other way after the U.S. provided secret papers, code-named Vesuvius, as proof that the Vietnamese were operating from his country.

While most Democratic and Republican hawks have praised the growing drone war in the skies over Pakistan, some experts in the U.S. are starting to express worries about them (even if they don't have the Cambodian analogy in mind). For example, John Arquilla, a professor of defense analysis at the Naval Postgraduate School who frequently advises the military, says that an expansion of the drone strikes "might even spark a social revolution in Pakistan."

Indeed, even Gen. David Petraeus, head of U.S. Central Command, wrote in a secret assessment on May 27, 2009: "Anti-U.S. sentiment has already been increasing in Pakistan ... especially in regard to cross-border and reported drone strikes, which Pakistanis perceive to cause unacceptable civilian casualties." Quoting local polls, he wrote: "35 percent [of Pakistanis] say they do not support U.S. strikes into Pakistan, even if they are coordinated with the GOP [government of Pakistan] and the Pakistan Military ahead of time."

The Pakistani army has, in fact, launched several significant operations against the Pakistani Taliban in Swat and in South Waziristan, just as Sihanouk initially ordered the Cambodian military to attack the Khmer Rouge and suppress peasant rebellions in Battambang Province. Again like Sihanouk in the late 1960s, however, the Pakistanis have balked at more comprehensive assaults on the Taliban, and especially on the Afghan Taliban using the border areas as "sanctuaries."

Pakistan May Be Destabilized

What happens next is the $64 million question. Most Pakistani experts dismiss any suggestion that the Taliban has widespread support in their country, but it must be remembered that the Khmer Rouge was a fringe group with no more than 4,000 fighters at the time that Operation Breakfast began.

And if Cambodia's history is any guide to the future, the drone strikes do not have to create a groundswell for revolution. They only have to begin to destabilize Pakistan as would, for instance, the threatened spread of such strikes into the already unsettled province of Baluchistan, or any future American ground incursions into the country. A few charismatic intellectuals like Khmer Rouge leader Pol Pot always have the possibility of taking it from there, rallying angry and unemployed youth to create an infrastructure for disruptive change.

Despite often repeated claims by both the Bush and Obama administrations that the drone raids are smashing al-Qaeda's intellectual leadership, more and more educated and disenchanted young men from around the world seem to be rallying to the fundamentalist cause.

Some have struck directly at American targets like Umar Farouk Abdulmutallab, the 23-year-old Nigerian who attempted to blow up a Detroit-bound plane on Christmas Day 2009, and Dr. Humam Khalil Abu Mulal al-Balawi, the 32-year-old Jordanian double agent and suicide bomber who killed seven CIA operatives at a military base in Khost, southern Afghanistan, five days later.

Some have even been U.S.-born, like Anwar al-Awlaki, the 38-year-old Islamic preacher from New Mexico who has moved to Yemen; Adam Pearlman, a 32-year-old Southern Californian and al-Qaeda spokesman now known as "Azzam the American," who reportedly lives somewhere in the Afghan-Pakistan border regions; and Omar Hammami, the 25-year-old Syrian-American from Alabama believed to be an al-Shabaab [a Somali Islamic insurgency group] leader in Somalia.

Like the Khmer Rouge before them, these new jihadists display no remorse for killing innocent civilians. "One of the sad truths I have come to see is that for this kind of mass violence, you don't need monsters," says Craig Etcheson, author of *After the Killing Fields* and founder of the Documentation Center of Cambodia. "Ordinary people will do just fine. This thing lives in all of us."

Even King Sihanouk, who had once ordered raids against the Khmer Rouge, eventually agreed to support them after he had been overthrown in a coup and was living in exile in China. Could the same thing happen to Pakistani politicians if they fall from grace and U.S. backing?

What threw Sihanouk's fragile government into serious disarray—other than his own eccentricity and self-absorption—was the devastating spillover of Nixon's war in Vietnam into Cambodia's border regions. It finally brought the Khmer Rouge to power.

Beware Secret Air Wars

Pakistan 2010, with its enormous modern military and industrialized base, is hardly impoverished Cambodia 1969. Nonetheless, in that now ancient history lies both a potential analogy and a cautionary tale. Beware secret air wars that promise success and yet wreak havoc in lands that are not even enemy nations.

When his war plans were questioned, Nixon pressed ahead, despite a growing public distaste for his war. A similar dynamic seems to be underway today. In 1970, after Operation Breakfast was revealed by the *New York Times*, Nixon told his top military and national security aides: "We cannot sit here and let the enemy believe that Cambodia is our last gasp."

Had he refrained first from launching Operation Breakfast and then from supping on the whole "menu," some historians like Etcheson believe a genocide would have been averted. It would be a sad day if the drone strikes, along with the endless war that the Obama administration has inherited and that is now spilling over ever more devastatingly into Pakistan, were to create a new class of fundamentalists who actually had the capacity to seize power.

> "The important lesson from the cap-
> ture of Baradar . . . is the improved co-
> operation between the ISI [Pakistan's
> intelligence service] and the CIA [U.S.
> Central Intelligence Agency] and the
> implications that this might have for
> the capture of Taliban leader Mullah
> Omar or al Qaeda leader Osama
> Bin Laden."

Military Cooperation Between the United States and Pakistan Can Help Defeat the Taliban

Eli Clifton and Charles Fromm

Eli Clifton and Charles Fromm are journalists whose work has appeared on Inter Press Service (IPS). *In the following view-point, they report on the capture in Pakistan of Abdul Ghani Baradar, an important Taliban commander. His capture, they say, is widely seen as a sign of improved relations between Ameri-can and Pakistani intelligence. If this is the case, they conclude, it could be a major step forward in the fight against the Taliban in Pakistan and Afghanistan.*

As you read, consider the following questions:

1. Who is Juan Cole, and under what circumstances does he believe that the capture of Abdul Ghani Baradar may be devastating to the Taliban?
2. According to the viewpoint, the Baradar capture comes in the midst of what?
3. What message do some analysts believe the Baradar capture may be sending to the Taliban in Pakistan?

The capture of Mullah Abdul Ghani Baradar last week [February 2010] in a joint operation conducted by the U.S. Central Intelligence Agency (CIA) and the Pakistani Inter-Services Intelligence (ISI) represents the most important Taliban leader to be taken into custody since the U.S. invasion of Afghanistan in 2001.

A Major Blow to the Taliban

The operation, which was conducted secretly in Karachi [Pakistan] last week, marks a major blow to the Taliban's leadership structure. Baradar was widely seen as the second in command under Taliban founder Mullah Muhammad Omar.

Baradar's capture occurred last week but the *New York Times* held off on reporting on the joint CIA and ISI operation at the request of the White House.

The White House has been uncharacteristically quiet about the operation, but a senior administration official told ABC news that, "This is a huge catch," and, "We haven't had something like this since the start of the war."

While refusing to discuss specifics of the operation, State Department Spokesman Gordon Duguid, told reporters, "I do, however, want to reemphasise that the United States and Pakistan work closely together on security issues in combating terrorism that threatens both of our societies. We have had a close relationship with the Pakistani government and I suspect that we will continue to work with them in pursuance of a policy that blunts the ability of extremist groups to attack both of our societies."

While the capture of Baradar, who was widely seen as the defacto leader of the Taliban insurgency, is a major boost to efforts by the U.S. and Pakistan to weaken the Taliban insurgency in Afghanistan and Pakistan, the successful operation also marks a change in the rocky CIA-ISI relationship.

The relationship between the two agencies has been one of distrust as the CIA has accused the ISI of maintaining contacts with senior Taliban leadership and the ISI has charged the CIA with faulty cooperation.

CIA and ISI cooperation on such a highly sensitive operation and the severe blow inflicted to the Taliban's leadership with the capture has led experts here in Washington to suggest that the operation may be a major victory for U.S. and Pakistani efforts to combat the Taliban insurgency.

"Depending on how much he is willing to reveal about the whereabouts and operational plans of the other Taliban commanders, his capture could be devastating for the Old Taliban," wrote University of Michigan history professor Juan Cole on his blog.

Improved Relations Between American and Pakistani Intelligence

But [global intelligence company] Stratfor's Reva Bhalla speculated in a CNN interview that, "It's hard to believe that this will lead to this huge intelligence coup, but if the Pakistanis are shifting their mode of cooperating [with the United States] that is significant."

Baradar's capture comes in the midst of a much heralded offensive by U.S. and Afghan forces in Marja, a Taliban stronghold in Afghanistan's southern Helmand province.

The Marja offensive has been held up as an example of the counterinsurgency (COIN) operations which will ulti-

Baradar's Duties

Baradar was ... in day-to-day charge of the insurgency; he also presided over the ruling Quetta Shura, the top policymaking body. He hired and fired provincial shadow governors as well as militia commanders. He controlled the insurgency's hefty treasury ... filled with the proceeds from kidnapping ransoms, tax receipts, protection rackets for the drug trade, and charitable donations from the Gulf nations.

Ron Moreau and Sami Yousafzai, "Next Up,"
Newsweek, *February 16, 2010. www.newsweek.com.*

mately determine the success or failure of the Obama administration's 30,000 troop surge in Afghanistan.

Baradar's role in the Afghan Taliban appears to have been pivotal in channeling donations from the Gulf to regional commanders in Afghanistan. The sums of money for which Baradar was ultimately responsible, according to some reports, exceeded the total Taliban revenue from trade and drug trade taxation.

Various scenarios have been discussed about what Baradar's capture means for the future of both Pakistani and Afghan negotiations with the Taliban.

Bhalla suggested that Baradar's capture may be a message from Pakistan, "telling Washington to deal with Islamabad— not Saudi Arabia—if it wants to negotiate with the Afghan Taliban."

Baradar is widely understood to have represented Taliban leader Mullah Omar in secret negotiations brokered by Saudi Arabia.

The BBC has cited sources in Pakistan that allege the arrest may have been "orchestrated" by elements within the ISI to aid back-channel talks with Taliban commanders who were willing to negotiate.

This suggests a scenario in which Baradar was walked in, rather than arrested in a raid, under a pre-arranged deal with the CIA to pave the way for negotiations.

Other analysts, such as the Afghanistan Analysts Network (AAN), and others, have received reports for several years that the ISI has pressured Taliban commanders to return to the battlefield inside Afghanistan or risk being handed over to the U.S. to be sent to Guantanamo Bay prison.

A scenario such as this would imply that the ISI arrested Baradar, sending the message to remaining Taliban members in Pakistan that they would no longer be granted sanctuary in Pakistan.

The important lesson from the capture of Baradar, according to many analysts, is the improved cooperation between the ISI and the CIA and the implications that this might have for the capture of Taliban leader Mullah Omar or [terrorist group] al Qaeda leader Osama Bin Laden.

"Pakistan's government must meet local needs and create jobs to address the causes of violence."

Pakistani Civilian Authorities, Not the Military, Must Address the Taliban Crisis

Shuja Nawaz

Shuja Nawaz is a Pakistani political and strategic analyst and director of the South Asia Center at the Atlantic Council. In the following viewpoint, he argues that Pakistan's civilian government needs to coordinate better with its military. Even if they do, though, he notes that military force alone cannot defeat the Taliban. Instead, he says, the Pakistan civilian government must reduce support for the insurgency by improving government and increasing economic opportunities. He also says the United States must do better in targeting its aid, and that it should include India in regional aid and development discussions.

Shuja Nawaz, "The Battle for Pakistan," *Wall Street Journal*, October 19, 2009. Copyright © 2009 Dow Jones & Company, Inc. All rights reserved. Reprinted with permission of The *Wall Street Journal*.

As you read, consider the following questions:

1. According to Nawaz, what happened after General Ash-faq Parvez Kayani briefed government opposition leaders on the deteriorating security situation in Pakistan and asked for direction?

2. What was the number of fatalities in the Pakistan/ Taliban conflict in 2003 and in 2009, according to Nawaz?

3. What sort of projects does Nawaz believe might be used to employ idle youth and drain the Taliban's recruitment pool?

Rising violence, targeted and random, has become a fact of life in Pakistan today [October 2009]. It threatens the country's political and economic future—and there still does not appear to be a strategy to stop it. The fledgling civilian government, composed of a weak coalition of opportunistic parties, has conceded to the military responsibility for organizing campaigns against insurgents who have set off a wave of attacks across the nation over the past two weeks.

The Government Is Disconnected from the Military

The latest military campaign in South Waziristan, launched Saturday, is a good example of the disconnect between the government and the military. The government has ceded all strategic authority to the army, and without civilian leadership, no military strategy can succeed there. It also reflects the continuation of a pattern that began soon after the Pakistan People's Party government succeeded the autocratic regime of President Pervez Musharraf last year. The then new army chief, Gen. Ashfaq Parvez Kayani, briefed the government opposition leaders on the deteriorating security situation and asked them to provide him with direction. He had to wait four weeks before being told to proceed with plans for clearing Taliban militants out of the Swat Valley [an area in northwest Pakistan].

The government eventually came up with slogans for countering terror and violence with "the 'three Ds' strategy of dialogue, development, and deterrence," as Prime Minister Yousaf Raza Gilani told the World Economic Forum at Davos [Switzerland] this year. But there has been little evidence on the ground of a practicable road map for achieving these goals.

Meanwhile the chart of death and destruction has been rising rapidly. This year [2009], the number of fatalities reached 8,375, up from 189 in 2003, according to the South Asia Terrorism Portal that tracks such figures from public records. Some 22,110 people were killed over the past six years, including at least 2,637 security personnel, 7,004 civilians and 5,960 terrorists or insurgents. The rise of the Tehrik-e-Taliban of Pakistan, a loose umbrella group of tribal factions based near the Afghan border, has added a new measure of danger. The Tehrik-e-Taliban also has ties with regional groups in the Federally Administered Tribal Areas and in the settled areas of Pakistan with the Punjabi militant groups (which were once trained by Pakistani intelligence to operate against India in Kashmir). These groups have begun targeting the army, culminating in the bold attack on army headquarters in Rawalpindi, near Islamabad, earlier this month.

The army is now in the middle of its offensive against the Tehrik-e-Taliban stronghold in the Mehsud territory of South Waziristan, a rugged and forbidding terrain where battle-hardened al Qaeda regulars have bolstered the group's numbers. It will be a tough and costly battle. If the army destroys the nucleus of the insurgent leadership in South Waziristan, it will have won a respite from the violence.

The War Will Continue

But the war will not be over. It is likely that Tehrik-e-Taliban and al Qaeda [a terrorist group] franchises in the Punjab will continue to wreak havoc in the hinterland cities where ineffective police cannot protect the population. As a reaction to the Waziristan campaign, the government this week closed down schools and other institutions that could be likely targets of attacks. And while the army will be able to clear centers of militancy, as it did in Swat earlier this year, it will likely not be equipped to hold the territory or build the local economy.

That is where the civilians need to step in. To date, they have been largely absent, and the militants are feeding off the local population's discontent with lack of governance and economic opportunities. In the Federally Administered Tribal Areas, for instance, where economic and social indicators reveal the region lags behind the rest of the country, female literacy is no more than 3%. Most of the so-called youth bulge [that is, a large young population group] there, some 300,000 people aged 16 to 25, is unemployed.

There does not appear to be hope on the horizon. Almost no U.S. assistance has reached the ground in these areas. It is also unclear whether the latest U.S. aid package of $1.5 billion a year for the next five years, passed by Congress last month, will trickle down to the needy. It probably won't, unless the U.S aid machinery is overhauled.

In the absence of robust civilian counterpart organizations, the army may need to be brought into the aid delivery loop initially, with due safeguards for monitoring the use of the assistance. Road works, dams and other infrastructure projects in Federally Administered Tribal Areas could rapidly provide employment to idle youth and drain the Taliban's recruitment pool. But so far none are planned. In North Waziristan last year, army commanders told me that they had expended their annual medical supplies just three months after setting up medical camps to treat civilians in remote locations.

Meet Local Needs

Pakistan's government must meet local needs and create jobs to address the causes of violence. At the national level, Mr. Gilani's government needs to focus sharply on delivering services and providing justice—not concentrate on clinging to power. If he fails, the democratic experiment may be threatened yet again, as it often has in Pakistan's fractured polity, where violence spawns civil unrest and then military intervention.

The U.S. and other friends of Pakistan must continue to support the development of an inclusive political system that allows all Pakistanis to participate in determining their political future. The family enterprises that dominate local politics and thrive on graft and preferred access to state resources cannot be supported. The U.S. would also do well to widen the aperture of its involvement in the region by bringing India into the picture. The strong, newly elected Congress Party-led government in New Delhi [the Indian capital] has the capacity to reduce potential tension on its neighbor's eastern frontier, allowing Pakistan to devote more troops to fighting militancy in its western region.

Longer term, if peace breaks out between India and Pakistan, the dividends will be widespread in both economies. Greater trade and a greater exchange of travelers will likely reduce hostility and shift the emphasis from military spending to civilian development and growth. That is the real answer to the growing violence in the region. But first, Islamabad has to take the reins.

Periodical Bibliography

The following articles have been selected to supplement the diverse views presented in this chapter.

Jayshree Bajoria   "Pakistan's New Generation of Terrorists," *Council on Foreign Relations*, May 6, 2010.

Daniel Byman   "Taliban vs. Predator," *Foreign Affairs*, March 18, 2009.

Michael Crowley   "Islamabad Boys," *The New Republic*, January 27, 2010.

Carlotta Gall and Eric Schmitt   "U.S. Questions Pakistan's Will to Stop Taliban," *New York Times*, April 23, 2009.

Kathy Kelly and Joshua Brollier   "Pressured from All Sides in Pakistan's Swat Valley," *Counterpunch*, May 17, 2010.

Mansur Khan Mahsud   "Who Is Hakimullah?" *The AfPak Channel— Foreign Policy*, April 29, 2010.

Shuja Nawaz   "At War With Pakistan's Taliban," *Atlantic Council*, July 14, 2009.

Fraser Nelson   "Don't Mention the Afghan-Pakistan War," *The Spectator*, July 26, 2008.

Erika Solomon   "Pakistani Taliban Claim Failed New York Bomb Attack," *Reuters*, May 2, 2010.

Sabrina Tavernise   "Killings Rattle Pakistan's Swat Valley," *New York Times*, April 22, 2010.

OPPOSING
VIEWPOINTS®
SERIES

CHAPTER 4

What Is the Taliban's Relationship with Other Nations?

Chapter Preface

India has been one of the most consistent opponents of the Taliban regime. Long an enemy of Muslim-majority Pakistan, and subject to Muslim terrorist attacks within its own borders, India has no desire to see a fundamentalist government established in nearby Afghanistan. Nor does India wish to see the Taliban gain influence in Pakistan. According to Stephen P. Cohen in his 2001 book *India: Emerging Power*, "if the Taliban should triumph in Afghanistan and spread its influence to Pakistan (or if Pakistan should gain control over the Taliban), India could be threatened by a revolutionary regime promulgating a dangerous religious message."

Because of its opposition to the Taliban, India has been very supportive of the Afghan government. After the Taliban were overthrown by the U.S. invasion in 2001, India "reached out to renew ties with Kabul [the capital of Afghanistan]. . . . Since 2001, India has offered $1.2 billion for Afghanistan's reconstruction, making it the largest regional donor to the country. By helping rebuild a new Afghanistan, India strives for greater regional stability, but also hopes to counter Pakistan's influence in Kabul, say experts. For India, Afghanistan is also a potential route for access to Central Asian energy," according to Jayshree Bajoria in a July 22, 2009, article on the Web site of the Council on Foreign Relations.

On one hand, India's support of Afghanistan can be seen as a move in its long-standing conflict with Pakistan. For example, Sanjeev Miglani, writing in a June 1, 2010, *Reuters* article, characterizes the Afghan conflict as "a proxy war between India and Pakistan," with India on the side of the Afghan government and forces in Pakistan supporting the Taliban.

On the other hand, however, the Afghan conflict can be seen as an opportunity for Pakistan and India to overcome their decades-long conflict in the interest of fighting a common foe. Since his election in 2008, "[Pakistani] President Asif Ali Zardari often has declared that Pakistan's single biggest challenge stems from 'religious' militants," such as the Taliban. "'India,' Zardari has said categorically, 'is not our enemy,'" according to Beena Sarwar, writing in a February 17, 2009, *IPS* article.

Whatever the impact of the Afghan conflict on Pakistan/India relations, it appears that India over time has decided that a more flexible approach to the Taliban is necessary. For a long time, India firmly opposed peace talks or negotiations with any Taliban elements. More recently, however, India has begun to support negotiations "in part to reduce the chances that Pakistan is able to play kingmaker in post-American Afghanistan," according to Robert Dreyfuss in a May 20, 2010, article on the *Nation* Web site. India wants to be part of peace negotiations, in short, because it wants to have influence in Afghanistan.

The following viewpoints look at the Taliban's interactions with other nations in the region and beyond, including Iran, China, Russia, and Saudi Arabia.

> *"From the Iranian point of view, this is the perfect time to demonstrate to the Americans that in addition to the Middle East, the Persian Islamist regime has great influence in South and Central Asia as well."*

Iran Opposes the Taliban

Strategic Forecasting, Inc. (STRATFOR)

Strategic Forecasting, Inc., or STRATFOR, is a global intelligence company. In the following viewpoint, STRATFOR argues that Iran plans to exert influence in Afghanistan by encouraging and allying with anti-Taliban ethnic groups, such as the Tajiks. The viewpoint suggests that Iran also may form links with Russia and India to oppose the Taliban. STRATFOR concludes that this anti-Taliban coalition may cause difficulties for the United States as it attempts to open negotiations with the Taliban.

As you read, consider the following questions:

1. What event occurred in 1998 in Mazar-e-Sharif, according to this viewpoint?

2. According to this viewpoint, what country is Iran's main regional rival, and why is that country interested in seeing the return of the Taliban?

"Afghanistan: The U.S. Between Iran and the Taliban," STRATFOR, March 21, 2009. Reproduced by permission.

3. Why does STRATFOR say that India is opposed to the Taliban?

Iranian Foreign Minister Manouchehr Mottaki arrived March 20 [2009] in the northwestern Afghan city of Mazar-e-Sharif to meet with his Afghan and Tajik counterparts in a ceremony marking Nowruz—the Persian New Year celebrated by Iranians, Tajiks, Kurds, and Azeris. On the same day, U.S. President Barack Obama sent a message to Iran on the occasion of Nowruz as part of his administration's efforts to engage Tehran [the capital of Iran] diplomatically.

Iran's Influence in Afghanistan

The Iranians have welcomed the "Happy Nowruz" message from Obama, but have reiterated their demand that the United States move beyond statements and take concrete steps to initiate the process of normalizing relations. Tehran knows that Washington is simultaneously trying to reach out to the clerical regime; it is also pursuing a diplomatic approach toward the Taliban, an enemy of Tehran that the Iranians nearly went to war with in 1998 [when the Taliban controlled Afghanistan—before they were overthrown by the United States in 2001]. From the Iranian point of view, this is the perfect time to demonstrate to the Americans that in addition to the Middle East, the Persian [that is, Iranian] Islamist regime has great influence in South and Central Asia as well.

Intriguingly, the regional gathering is not being held in the Afghan capital, Kabul, but in Mazar-e-Sharif—a city with a Tajik majority in a predominantly Uzbek region, which is near the borders of the Central Asian states (Turkmenistan, Uzbekistan and Tajikistan). It is also the same city where the Taliban murdered 10 diplomats and an Iranian journalist at the Iranian Consulate in August 1998 as part of a larger massacre of Shiite [a religious branch of Islam, including most Iranians] opponents in and around the town after the Taliban re-

Iran/Afghan Ties

Iran has close linguistic and cultural ties to Afghanistan, particularly with Tajiks. . . . In modern times, [Iranian capital] Tehran's role has often aligned with U.S. interests. Iran opened its borders to millions of Afghan refugees during the war against the Soviet Union in the 1980s. Later in the 1990s it worked with various mujahadeen groups, including the Northern Alliance . . . , to undermine Soviet influence and later Taliban rule. After the Taliban took power in 1996, Iran's supreme leader denounced the group as an affront to Islam, and the killing of eleven Iranian diplomats and truck drivers in 1998 almost triggered a military conflict.

Greg Bruno, *"Iran and the Future of Afghanistan,"*
Council on Foreign Relations, *March 30, 2009. www.cfr.org.*

captured it from the Northern Alliance. Ethnic Tajiks, Uzbeks, Hazara and Turkmen in Afghanistan, along with their allies in Asghabat, Tashkent and Dushanbe all share Iran's deep concern over the Taliban resurgence. These state and non-state actors, along with Russia, Iran and India, cooperated in supporting the Northern Alliance (a coalition of Afghan minorities) to counter the Taliban from 1994 to 2001 and then played an instrumental role in the fall of the Taliban regime in the aftermath of 9/11 [the September 11, 2001, terrorist attacks on the United States].

Iran, Russia, and India

Tehran has strong influence among Afghanistan's largest minority group, the Tajiks, because of ethnolinguistic ties. Similarly, it enjoys close relations with the Hazara, who are—like the Iranians—Shia. Given the way the Taliban routed the

Northern Alliance in the 1990s, the Iranians understand that they will need to put together a more robust alliance comprising the Afghan minorities. The Uzbeks, however, are key in this regard because after the Tajiks, they are the next-largest ethnic group in the country. Moreover, the Uzbeks under the leadership of former military commander Gen. Abdul-Rashid Dostum played a key role in the ouster of the Marxist regime [allied with the former Soviet Union, which fought to control Afghanistan through the 1980s] in 1992 after defecting to the Islamist rebel alliance.

Therefore, in addition to showing off their regional influence, the Iranians are likely attempting to revive the Northern Alliance. In April 2007, STRATFOR discussed the likelihood of the re-creation of the north-south divide in Afghanistan, pitting its Pashtun majority [the ethnic group from which most of the Taliban come] against the country's minorities. By countering the rise of the Taliban, the Iranians would be off-setting the moves of their main regional rival, Saudi Arabia. Riyadh [the capital of Saudi Arabia] is interested in seeing the return of the Taliban as a means of checking Iran, which has created problems for Riyadh in the Arab world. Just as Iran has relied on its Arab Shiite allies and other radical forces in the Middle East to expand its influence, the Iranians have ample tools on their eastern front.

Iran is not the only power that has an interest in bolstering the Northern Alliance. The Russians also want to keep the Taliban contained, and would have an interest in undermining U.S. strategy in Afghanistan by reinforcing the Taliban's biggest rivals. Iran will probably work through Russia to create a regional alliance against the Taliban, though Iran is aware that Moscow [capital of Russia] does not want Iran to expand its influence in Central Asia because the Russians see that region as their exclusive turf.

Additionally, Iran can rely on India to join this anti-Taliban regional alliance because of [Indian capital] New Delhi's interest in countering the Taliban's main state-actor ally, Pakistan, and countering the Islamist militant threat that India faces from its western rival [that is, Pakistan]. The Indians have openly criticized U.S. efforts to seek out "moderate" Taliban and are bitter about the Obama administration's soft approach toward Islamabad [the Pakistan capital].

A Complicated Situation

This emerging alignment of forces complicates an already complex and difficult situation that the United States faces in dealing with Taliban and their al Qaeda [a terrorist group] allies. Washington is struggling to deal with the spread of the jihadist [Islamic fundamentalist] insurgency from Afghanistan to Pakistan and now will have to balance between Iran and Saudi Arabia as it seeks to deal with the Taliban. A revitalization of an anti-Taliban alliance of state and non-state actors will create problems for the U.S. efforts to negotiate with the Taliban.

Such an anti-Taliban coalition also complicates U.S.-NATO [North Atlantic Treaty Organization] efforts to reach out to the Central-Asian republics and Russia in its search for alternative supply routes. Moscow and the Central Asian states are in favor, at the right price, of allowing the West to ship supplies through their territories to NATO forces in Afghanistan because they also want the Taliban in check. Washington's moves to talk to the Taliban, however, are a cause of concern for the Kremlin [Russian government] and the countries of Central Asia, which is why they will be asking for a role in the U.S.-Iranian negotiations.

These complex dealings underscore the problems that the United States will be facing as it seeks simultaneously to negotiate with its two principal opponents in the Islamic world— Iran and the jihadists.

"The presence of Chinese weapons so close to the Iranian border is the strongest evidence to date suggesting Tehran has had at least an indirect role in arms shipments to Afghanistan."

The Taliban May Be Obtaining Chinese Weapons from Iran

Ron Synovitz

Ron Synovitz is a senior correspondent in the newsroom of Radio Free Europe/Radio Liberty. In the following viewpoint, he reports that Chinese weapons shipped to Iran have been showing up in the possession of Taliban fighters. Synovitz says that the United States claims that Iran may be involved in providing the Taliban with weapons. The number of weapons makes it likely that someone in the Iranian state apparatus knows about the shipments, Synovitz reports. On the other hand, Synovitz says, Iranian self-interest and its ties to the Afghan government make it seem unlikely, and difficult to prove, that Iran is intentionally sending weapons to the Taliban.

Ron Synovitz, "Afghanistan: U.S. Worried Iran Sending Chinese Weapons to Taliban," *Radio Free Europe/Radio Liberty*, September 14, 2007. Copyright © 2007 RFE/RL, Inc. All rights reserved. Reprinted with the permission of *Radio Free Europe/Radio Liberty*, 1201 Connecticut Ave., N.W. Washington DC 20036. www.rferl.org.

As you read, consider the following questions:

1. What weapons were in the cache found in Ghurian district, according to Synovitz?
2. According to the author, at what point did Iran and the Taliban become firm enemies?
3. Who does analyst Alex Vatanka suggest that Iran might be supplying instead of the Taliban?

U.S. Deputy Secretary of State John Negroponte says Washington has complained to [Chinese capital] Beijing about Chinese weapons shipments to Iran that appear to be turning up in the hands of Taliban fighters in Afghanistan.

From China to Iran to the Taliban

Negroponte confirmed the U.S. concerns over China's weapons deals with Tehran after a 10-ton weapons cache was discovered in the western Afghan province of Herat.

The cache found in Ghurian district, near the border with Iran, included artillery shells, land mines, and rocket-propelled grenade launchers with Chinese, Russian, and Persian markings on them.

Britain's Foreign Office has also confirmed that it has complained to Beijing about Chinese-made HN-5 antiaircraft missiles confiscated from Taliban fighters who were captured or killed by British Royal Marines in Helmand Province. Beijing has said that it would investigate allegations that the weapons were forwarded to the Taliban through Iran.

When asked in Kabul [the capital of Afghanistan] on September 11 [2007] about the Taliban's use of sophisticated new Chinese weapons, U.S. Deputy Secretary of State John Negroponte also suggested that Iran has been a transit point for Chinese arms deliveries to the Taliban.

"A subject that I have discussed with the Chinese in the past is the fact of their weapons sales to the country of Iran and our concern," Negroponte said. "We have tried to discourage the Chinese from signing any new weapons contracts with Iran. We are concerned by reports—which we consider to be reliable—of explosively formed projectiles and other kinds of military equipment coming from Iran across the border and coming into the hands of the Taliban."

In June, U.S. Secretary of Defense Robert Gates said Washington had no evidence proving a direct role by the Iranian government in smuggling weapons to the Taliban. But Gates said Washington suspects Tehran [the Iranian capital] is involved.

"I haven't seen any intelligence specifically to this effect, but I would say, given the quantities we are seeing, it is difficult to believe that it is associated with smuggling or the drug business or that it is taking place without the knowledge of the Iranian government," Gates said.

Tehran May Know

Alex Vatanka is the Washington-based Iran analyst for Jane's Information Group, which publishes *Jane's Defence Weekly* and other journals about the weapons industry and global security issues. Vatanka says it will remain unclear whether the Ghurian weapons cache is linked to the Taliban until Afghan or U.S. authorities announce details of their joint investigation.

But the presence of Chinese weapons so close to the Iranian border is the strongest evidence to date suggesting Tehran has had at least an indirect role in arms shipments to Afghanistan.

"Whether the government or somebody in Iran could be buying arms from China and, without Tehran's knowledge, ship it over to Afghanistan—on that volume of weapons—I find that extremely unlikely," Vatanka says.

"I can only see that happening if somebody pretty senior and in an influential political position in Iran decided to facilitate that without letting everybody in the system know about it," he continues. "But they still had to be involved somewhere in the state machinery. We're not talking about rogue elements [in Iran]. Baluchi [an ethnic group in Southeast Iran by the Afghan border] drug traffickers can't pull that kind of thing off."

Many analysts have noted that Shi'ite Iran and the Sunni Taliban [the Shiite and Sunni are rival Islamic sects] had been firm enemies since 1998, when the Taliban regime controlled most of Afghanistan and executed nine Iranian diplomats in Mazar-e Sharif.

But Pakistani journalist Ahmed Rashid, an expert on Islamic militancy in the region and author of the book *Taliban*, says that times appear to have changed. Now, with U.S. forces deployed some 60 kilometers from the Iranian border at Shindad Airfield in Herat Province, Rashid says Tehran and the Taliban have a common enemy.

"I have no doubt that Iran has been involved in channeling money and arms to various elements in Afghanistan, including the Taliban, for the last few years. They have long-running relations with many of the commanders and small-time warlords in western Afghanistan," Rashid says. "I think Iran is playing all sides in the Afghan conflict. And there are Pashtuns [the majority ethnic group in Afghanistan, from which most of the Taliban are drawn] and non-Pashtuns who are being funded by Iran who are active in western Afghanistan. If the Iranians are convinced that the Americans are undermining them through western Afghanistan, then it is very likely that these agents of theirs have been activated."

Political Backlash

Still, Vatanka says it would be "almost irrational behavior" for Tehran to supply the Taliban with weapons. He says such a move would almost certainly lead to a negative domestic political backlash for Iranian President Mahmud Ahmadinejad's government.

For that reason, Vatanka says he is eagerly awaiting the assessment of Afghan and U.S. investigators about whether the arms in the Ghurian cache were stashed away by the Taliban or by one of several rival militia factions in Herat Province.

"The question is, what would get even a faction within Iran to make that type of a decision? Maybe you have excellent business ties between the Iranians and the Afghans on the other side—not necesarily the central government in Kabul—but local leaders in Herat who turn around saying, 'You Iranians are building roads and infrastructure here. You are setting up shops and factories. But for us to be able to guarantee that we can protect your business interests, we'll need to receive some arms.' That's an argument that one could put out: that the Iranians are essentially supplying not the Taliban, but Afghan partners to secure Iranian businesses and interests in western Afghanistan," Vatanka says.

To date, Afghan President Hamid Karzai has refused to publicly support allegations of a direct link between Tehran and weapons shipments to the Taliban. "We don't have any such evidence so far of the involvement of the Iranian government in supplying the Taliban. We have a very good relationship with the Iranian government. Iran and Afghanistan have never been as friendly as they are today," Karzai has said.

Vatanka says that as long as Karzai maintains that position, skeptics around the world will dismiss suggestions from Washington that Tehran is supplying Taliban fighters in Afghanistan.

"From a U.S. point of view, if the insurgency in Afghanistan is essentially escalating based on Iranian assistance, then what Washington really needs to do is to provide far more evidence that points to that—and get Mr. Hamid Karzai in Kabul and the regional governments in Afghanistan to back the U.S. up when it makes these claims against Iran," Vatanka says.

After the U.S. military failed to find the weapons of mass destruction allegedly being stockpiled in Iraq, [following the U.S. invasion of Iraq in 2003] Vatanka says, "the skeptics out there are saying, 'These [new allegations] are being made up by the U.S. to justify another war with Iran'—which might not actually be the case. Iran might be involved. But because of the lack of evidence, the Iranians are saying, 'Who else is backing up the U.S. allegations?'"

"The reason for Russia and China's concern over Central Asia is not US might, but actually its weakness."

Russia and China Are Working to Contain the Taliban

Dmitry Shlapentokh

Dmitry Shlapentokh is an associate professor of history at Indiana University South Bend. In the following viewpoint, he argues that the U.S. economic crisis forces it to abandon the war in Afghanistan. He notes that China and Russia are both nervous about the prospect of a Taliban victory leading to Muslim insurgencies throughout Central Asia, which could in turn increase violence and disrupt gas pipelines. Thus, China and Russia have formed an uneasy alliance to work against the Taliban, although Shlapentokh says the ultimate success of that alliance is uncertain.

As you read, consider the following questions:

1. According to Shlapentokh, what bankruptcy shows that the U.S.'s economic foundations are eroding?

Dmitry Shlapentokh, "China, Russia Face Up to Taliban Threat," *Asia Times*, May 15, 2009. Copyright © 2009 Asia Times Online Ltd. All rights reserved. Reproduced by permission. www.atimes.com.

2. Why, according to the author, is Tajikistan unwilling to form an alliance with Russia?

3. Why would Central Asian states be even less pleased with a Chinese presence than with a Russian one, according to Shlapentokh?

R ussian President Dmitry Medvedev announced in April [2009] that Russia and China would strengthen their military cooperation through the Shanghai Cooperative Organization (SCO), and engage in several joint military maneuvers.

U.S. Decline

Some observers feel the plans for improved ties are aimed at limiting the United States' presence in Central Asia, but there are more factors in play. The new promises of cooperation are not based solely on fear of the West's imperial expansion, as was the case in 2001 at the beginning of the [U.S. President] George W Bush and [Russian President] Vladimir Putin presidencies.

Indeed, 2009 is very different from 2001, when the US— full of confidence as the only superpower and taking advantage of the September 11, 2001, attacks—accelerated a drive for imperial expansion that had begun in the late 1980s when the Soviet empire started to crumble. Now, it is the US's turn for a decline, and it could be a rapid one.

The erosion of the US's economic foundations is clear. Chrysler, one of the major US car companies, is bankrupt, and its other major car manufacturers are moving in the same direction. Even the most optimistic economists are assuming that recovery from the financial crisis will be slow and that unemployment will remain high in the foreseeable future.

President Barack Obama has made some sound statements in regard to the improvement of the US economy in the long run, such as increasing reliance on alternate forms of energy and the development of the country's railroads. Still, unless his goal is a Potemkin Village [that is, fake] showcase with no visible implications for the US economy, he needs more than some elements of a planned economy. Nothing like this is in sight; and the US mint will continue to print billions of dollars and the country's debt continues to pile up.

The economic decline is increasingly being translated into military weakness, which will affect US military operations in Iraq and Afghanistan. With mercenary armies increasingly employed, the military is inspired not so much by the image of the flag as the image of cash. And this is increasingly short in supply. The endless redeployment of the same soldiers also leads to poor morale.

While the US is in the process of decline, it has considerably reduced its tensions with Russia. The US-China relationship is also much better than in 2001, when there was the serious incident over the American spy plane that collided with a Chinese fighter over China's air space.

U.S. Weakness Is the Danger

The reason for Russia and China's concern over Central Asia is not US might, but actually its weakness. Both nations fear that the coming surge of US troops in Afghanistan might be the last desperate attempt to turn the tide before departure, which would lead to the spread of Muslim insurgencies not just in Pakistan but in Central Asia. This increased spread of Muslim insurgents could not only disrupt the gas and oil supply from the region, which is essential for both China and Russia, but create problems in their respective Muslim-dominated areas.

Russia is increasingly concerned with the deteriorating situation in Afghanistan, which led to its attempt to build a sort of united force with Central Asian states as well as other former republics of the Soviet Union, such as Belarus. It soon became obvious that those arrangements will have little value.

Alexander Lukashenko, the Belarusian leader, stated that he would not send troops outside Belarus, while Uzbekistan's President Islam Karimov lost interest in military cooperation with Russia early on. The same seems to be true with Tajikistan's President Emomali Rahmon.

Despite the country's vulnerability due to its proximity to Afghanistan, the Tajik press increasingly presents Russia in an unfriendly light. Not only is Russia accused of sending back Tajik migrant workers, but also of not providing Tajikistan with enough economic assistance. Russia is also accused of fomenting the Tajik civil war in the 1990s.

With their plans for alliances in Central Asia flagging, Russia turned to China as the only option; and China seemed to be happy to reciprocate. Still, Russia continues to be suspicious of China because it is economically stronger and has greater demographic clout in the Far East.

China also does not see Russia as a trusted ally. China does not receive Russian gas or oil in its entirety and competes with Russia for Central Asia's natural resources. China was also displeased with the Russian war in Georgia, the ultimate goal of "regime change" in Tblisi [the capital of Georgia] and Russia's recognition of the breakaway Georgian regions Abkahazia and South Ossetia.

The Central Asian states, despite their suspicion and dislike of Russia, could well be even more displeased with a strong Chinese presence in their region, because of the fear that China with its huge population and rising economic and military muscle could totally absorb Central Asia in the future. While possibly all states in the region understand the danger of the Taliban in various degrees, it remains to be seen if the Chinese/Russian cooperation will, indeed, stop the Taliban tide.

> *"Supporters in Saudi Arabia and Kuwait provide perhaps as much income for the Taliban as drug sales."*

Money from Individuals in Russia and Saudi Arabia Helps Support the Taliban

Ryan Mauro

Ryan Mauro is the founder of WorldThreats.com and the author of Death to America: The Unreported Battle of Iraq. *In the following viewpoint, he argues that the Taliban are becoming a criminal network as much as a terrorist one, and that much of their funding comes from criminal activities. He also notes that the Taliban receive significant funding from individuals in Saudi Arabia and Russia. Part of this foreign funding, he says, comes from those who support the Taliban's Islamist cause, but part, especially in Russia, comes from those who are connected to the Taliban's organized criminal activities.*

As you read, consider the following questions:

1. Why does Mauro say that the Swat Valley is financially important to the Taliban?

Ryan Mauro, "Stopping the Taliban Mafia," *Front Page Magazine*, June 1, 2009. Copyright © 2009 FrontPageMagazine.com. Reproduced by permission.

2. Why does the drop in Afghan opium cultivation not indicate progress in the fight against the Taliban according to Mauro?

3. Who is Viktor But?

As the world waits to see if the Pakistani military has the will and the ability to save the country from the Taliban, an equally pressing question confronts the international community: How can the Taliban's funding sources be located and severed in order to prevent them from becoming the first nuclear-armed terrorist group?

A Hybrid Terrorist Mafia

In an interview last week [May 2009], General David Petraeus said that the Taliban is being funded with "hundreds and hundreds of millions of dollars" annually from drugs, foreign donations, and "locally generated" sources of income, particularly organized crime. As their responsibility for up to a third of the bank robberies in Karachi [Pakistan] in recent years shows, the Taliban has become a hybrid terrorist mafia.

A Pakistani intelligence report says that militants under the command of Baitullah Mehsud, the head of the Pakistani Taliban engage in "criminal activities like kidnapping for ransom, bank robbery, street robbery and other heinous crimes" to help finance their activities. Some companies owned by members of the Mehsud tribe in Pakistan are paying 40 percent of their income to the Taliban, sometimes by force and sometimes of their own accord. The sale of cigarettes and salvaged vehicles are other business investments.

The Swat Valley, the site of the current Pakistani military offensive following the Islamists' establishment of Sharia Law [Islamic law], is exceedingly important for the Taliban. Not only was it a safe haven for extremists, but its emerald mines and timber were good business. A Taliban spokesperson in the Swat Valley confirmed in April [2009] that they received one-third of the profit from the emerald mines, which are said to be bringing the Taliban at least $3 million annually, an amount that increases as more mines are utilized.

The Taliban also use the money from the mines to maintain local support. The Taliban spokesperson said the rest of the profit goes to the workers. During the takeover of one mine near Swat Valley, the Taliban told the mineworkers that they'd receive half the profit.

It is also cheap for the Taliban to operate in Karachi because of the support of local Pashtuns [the ethnic group from which most Taliban are drawn] that sometimes hold secret fundraisers for them. Tribes in Kandahar, Afghanistan, also provide Taliban operatives with funding for medical treatment, food, fuel, and other expenses. The Taliban benefit from the tribes' local culture, which requires "taking care of their own," as explained by one *Asia Times* reporter who sat in on a fundraising meeting in Karachi that brought in over $11,600.

The drug trafficking element of the Taliban's fundraising has been widely covered. The United Nations [U.N.] Drug Office believes the Taliban made up to $300 million from opium sales in 2008. Money is not only made from the sales, but from also charging "protection fees" for those moving the drugs over the Afghanistan borders and for the drug laboratories. Afghan opium cultivation in 2008 fell nearly 20 percent, and production fell six percent. However, according to Antonio Maria Costa, the executive director of the U.N. Drug Office, this does not reflect progress by those fighting the Taliban. The Taliban has simply produced so much that they have reduced cultivation and are stockpiling current supplies to artificially keep prices higher.

Foreign Funding

The focus on the Taliban's organized crime activity shouldn't distract from the need to stop foreign funding of the group. Supporters in Saudi Arabia and Kuwait provide perhaps as

The Taliban and Organized Crime

The police [in Karachi, Pakistan] say the Taliban ... are using Mafia-style networks to kidnap, rob banks and extort, generating millions of dollars ...

These criminal syndicates helped drive kidnappings in Pakistan last year to their highest numbers in a decade, ... and they have also generated a spike in bank robberies. Eighty percent of bank heists are now believed to be related to the insurgency and other militant groups.

Sabrina Tavernise, "Organized Crime in Pakistan Feeds Taliban,"
New York Times, August 28, 2009. www.nytimes.com.

much income for the Taliban as drug sales. The United Arab Emirates is another hot-spot for the Taliban, with the late high-level commander Mullah Dadullah reportedly visiting the country in early 2006.

Most of this foreign funding comes from an unofficial network called *hawala*, which is often used in countries that don't have a functioning banking system. An estimated $13–17 billion is transferred through *hawala* each year. Free of any signed documents, fees, regulation, or recording mechanisms and minimal delays, *hawala* is a cheap and attractive system for criminals, terrorists, or even average citizens.

If Justice Salam, who served on the Taliban's Supreme Court, is to be believed, then private citizens in the Arab world and Pakistan are not the only foreign financiers of the Taliban. He claims that the intelligence services of Pakistan, Iran, and, most surprisingly, Russia, are also providing financing as well as weapons. These three countries have also been singled out for assisting the Taliban by no less an authority that the Taliban's former deputy chief of finance.

Hamid Mir, a Pakistani reporter who has significant contacts in the Taliban and Al-Qaeda [a terrorist organization] and is the only journalist to have interviewed Osama Bin Laden [the leader of al Qaeda] after 9/11 [the September 11, 2001, terrorist attacks on the United States], told me the same thing in 2006. He accused Iran and Russia of supporting the Taliban, saying that "Russia is covertly supporting Taliban insurgents in Afghanistan. The spokesman of the Afghan Interior Ministry, Lutaffulah Mashal, told me in September 2005 in Kabul [the capital of Afghanistan] that the Taliban are getting modern Russian-made weapons. He suspected that Russia may be taking revenge on the U.S. for supporting the Afghan Mujahideen against Russia in the 1980s."

It is more likely that the alleged Russian assistance to the Taliban does not come from direct government orders, but from the activity of the Russian mafia working with corrupt officials. One such Russian criminal is Viktor But, a former high-level Soviet officer "suspected of being the main gunrunner to al-Qaida and the Taliban" who said in 2002 that he was living in Russia without any action being taken by the authorities. He was ultimately arrested on February 6, 2008 in Thailand.

In the battle against the Taliban, the struggle against terrorists and the struggle against organized crime have become intertwined. As the Taliban loses support among the Pakistani population, it will morph into an Islamist mafia, relying upon bribes and force to sustain itself. Defeating the Taliban will not only require a Pakistani military presence to free the locals from fear, but competent law enforcement and an international effort to better regulate the *hawala* networks that will enable criminals and terrorists to operate for years to come.

"The Saudis say they are friends of the West and of all Muslim nations, but their real alliance is with Iran, Hamas and the Taliban."

Saudi Arabia Tacitly Supports the Taliban

Rachel Ehrenfeld

Rachel Ehrenfeld is director of the American Center for Democracy and author of Funding Evil: How Terrorism Is Financed and How to Stop It. *In the following viewpoint, she argues that Saudi Arabia has provided little aid to victims of Taliban violence in Pakistan while providing a great deal of aid to Palestine. Ehrenfeld says this indicates that Saudi Arabia is interested in supporting radical Islam, and that it has joined with Iran to promote an Islamic world-government.*

As you read, consider the following questions:

1. In the four months after January 2009, how much money did Saudi Arabia and the Gulf States give to the Palestinians, according to Ehrenfeld?

2. What does Ehrenfeld say that Saudi Arabia gave to suffering Pakistanis as humanitarian aid in April 2009?

Rachel Ehrenfeld, "Where Is Saudi Support for Taliban Victims?" *Forbes*, May 12, 2009. Copyright © 2009 Forbes, Inc. Reproduced by permission.

3. What is the *ummah*?

Conspicuously, neither Saudi Arabia's King Abdullah bin Abdulaziz nor the rulers of any Arab or Muslim state are holding special national telethons to help raise funds for some 400,000 new Pakistani refugees. Many fled their homes after the Taliban took over the Swat valley, and others were forced to leave amid the fierce fighting between the Taliban and the Pakistani military. The Saudis say they are friends of the West and of all Muslim nations, but their real alliance is with Iran, Hamas and the Taliban—as you can tell just by following the money.

Indeed, to get hundreds of millions, and even billions, of dollars in emergency funds from Saudi Arabia, Kuwait and the Gulf States, the Pakistani refugees should have declared themselves Palestinian.

Since January 2009, or in just over four months, Saudi Arabia and the Gulf States have given between $1.646 billion and $1.950 billion to the Palestinians, according to figures published on the Web site of Saudi Arabia's embassy in the U.S.

Most of the money, as well as medical aid, food and building materials, went to Hamas-controlled Gaza. These donations were in addition to $1 billion donated on Jan. 19 by King Abdullah "to help rebuild the Gaza Strip."

On May 6, a day after U.S. Defense Secretary Robert Gates sought Saudi help to fight off the Taliban in Pakistan, the Saudis announced a $25 million donation, not to Pakistan, but to rebuild the Palestinian Nahr Al-Bared refugee camp in Lebanon.

Meanwhile on May 7, at the Arab League's meeting of foreign ministers in Cairo, Egypt, aid to Pakistan was not on the agenda. Instead, as reported by the *Saudi Gazette*, the League issued a warning about the imminent danger posed to Jerusalem by the Jews.

On May 10, while a new influx of 100,000 Pakistanis escaped the fighting between the military and the Taliban, Saudi Interior Minister Prince Naif, Saudi Foreign Minister Prince Saud Al-Faisal, chairman of the Kingdom Holding Company Prince Alwaleed bin Talal, and Gulf Cooperation Council (GCC) Secretary-General Abdul Rahman Al-Attiyah all found the time to meet with Sri Lankan Foreign Minister Rohitha Bogollagama. They promised to send a high-level delegation "to consider the volume of assistance that could be rendered to rehabilitate the [internal] refugees" in war-torn Sri Lanka.

So what about Saudi aid to the suffering Pakistanis? On April 23, the Saudi King gave Pakistan 150 tons of dates, as "humanitarian aid."

Is this an appropriate response from the "custodian" of the two holiest mosques, the second-largest Muslim country in the world and one that is 70% Sunni?

The Saudis are pouring money into Gaza, where Iranian-supported, *sharia*-forcing Hamas caused death and destruction. At the same time, they are avoiding supporting Pakistan against the Iranian-supported, *sharia*-enforcing, murderous Taliban.

It seems that the Saudis care more about enforcement of the most radical form of *sharia* as imposed by Hamas and the Taliban, than they do about helping hundreds of thousands of suffering Muslim brothers in Pakistan.

Support to Hamas and the indirect endorsement of the Taliban are a telling sign of important changes in the Muslim world. The Sunni-Wahhabi Saudis and the Shiite radicals ruling Iran seem to have put aside their differences for now. The uniting factor is the opportunity to speed up the creation of the global Islamic nation—the *ummah* in Arabic.

The Taliban, like Hamas, achieved political and territorial gains by brute force. Hamas threw the Fatah-run Palestinian Authority out of the Gaza Strip, and the Taliban took over Pakistan's Swat valley, through relentless terrorist attacks. Both terrorist groups received tactical and strategic support from Iran and funds from the Saudis.

On April 28, former head of Saudi intelligence Prince Turki al-Faisal, who admitted funding the Taliban before 9/11 and who served as ambassador to Washington, was quoted in the *Washington Times* calling for "the speedy withdrawal of U.S. and NATO forces from Afghanistan," saying that they are "not welcome" there.

Pakistan's decision to cede power over the Swat Valley to the Taliban, and the Obama administration's decision to talk with Hamas and Iran, only help to bolster these groups' demands and increase their influence in the Arab and Muslim world. The more concessions the West makes to radical Islam, the stronger it gets and the closer it comes to the Islamic dream—and the rest of the world's nightmare—of the coming *ummah*.

> *"The entrance of Saudi's King Abdul-*
> *lah as acting arbiter . . . serves as a*
> *game-changer in the US-Afghanistan*
> *seven-year stalemate."*

Saudi Arabia Could Act as an Arbiter with the Taliban

Michael Shank

Michael Shank is a former communications director at George Mason University's Institute for Conflict Analysis and Resolution. In the following viewpoint, he argues that Saudi Arabia's apparent willingness to act as mediator with the Taliban could offer a way out of the stalemated conflict in Afghanistan. Shank suggests that a move toward peace would make it possible for Afghanistan to address many of its pressing economic problems. He adds that Saudi-brokered peace talks also could help America begin to shift from military to development aid for Afghanistan.

As you read, consider the following questions:

1. What does Shank say that U.S. defense secretary Robert Gates has finally acknowledged?

2. According to Shank, how much of every U.S. dollar spent on Afghanistan is committed to non-military assistance?

3. What are the unemployment and literacy rates in Afghanistan, according to Shank?

Wandering seven long years [as of 2008] in the mountains and deserts of Afghanistan with hardly an end in sight, the US has just been offered a most fortuitous fix. It likely eludes America's current president [George W. Bush] and queuing candidates, [Democrat] Barack Obama and [Republican] John McCain, but not for long.

An End to the Stalemate

The fix is found in Mecca, Saudi Arabia. Long considered the most stable of US allies in the Middle East, the Kingdom appeared last week [October 2008] best positioned to play a leadership role in the region after hosting a series of non-official talks between Afghanistan's oppositional leaderships: those formally sanctioned in Kabul [Afghanistan's capital] under [Afghan President] Hamid Karzai and those informally sanctioned, yet arguably equally powerful, under the Taliban.

Just as Qatar's [the capital of Saudi Arabia] good offices ably brought Beirut's [that is, Lebanon's] embattled to the table to turn stalemate into starting point, Saudi Arabia can similarly serve as intercessor here.[1]

Talks with the Taliban were never a non-starter with the Afghan government, nor is Kabul's careful communicative overture new. The Afghan ambassador to the US, whom I interviewed this spring, cited "different degrees of engagement [with the Taliban] right now" and reaffirmed Kabul's continued willingness to communicate. This tone and tactic has long been untenable for the US administration, and so Afghanistan has been left to its own dialogical devices.

1. Saudi Arabia facilitated peace talks between Lebanese factions in 2008.

But now even Robert Gates, the US secretary of defence, acknowledges that talks with the Taliban are necessary. "There has to be ultimately, and I'll underscore ultimately, reconciliation as part of a political outcome to this," Gates said last Thursday [October 2008]. "That's ultimately the exit strategy for all of us."

The entrance of Saudi's King Abdullah as acting arbiter, therefore, serves as a game-changer in the US-Afghanistan seven-year stalemate. Not only would Saudi-officiated talks save US face from a seeming capitulation, but Mecca is measurably more meritorious as neutral ground than Kabul could ever be.

Suppose talks ensue. Will this suffice, as some speculate, in severing linkages with [terrorist group] al-Qaida, taming the Taliban, or solving the country's internal haemorrhaging? Surely not, but it will begin to force accountability among Afghanistan's feuding politicos, leverage a more effective hand in dealing with Pakistan and ameliorate the misguided modus operandi of foreign forces.

Non-Military Solutions Are Needed

This last point is of particular importance. America's current solution to Afghanistan's insecurity is solidly military, while political and economic solutions, not unlike in Iraq, are put on the backburner by Washington. Less than a dime of every US dollar spent on the country is committed to non-military assistance. This Bush doctrine under the leadership of [Secretary of State] Condoleezza Rice will soon become the Obama or McCain doctrine, as projected aid by both candidates has amounted to no greater a percentage. Yet after seven years of a predominantly military mission, Joint Chief of Staff Admiral Mike Mullen stated in September his doubts as to whether the US is winning.

Clearly a change in tack is necessary, but in what direction?

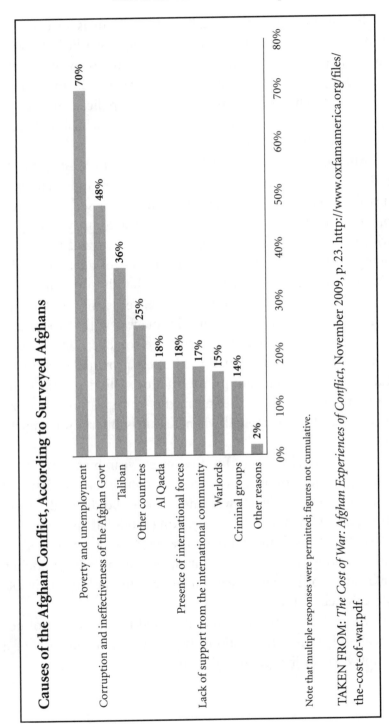

Causes of the Afghan Conflict, According to Surveyed Afghans

Cause	Percentage
Poverty and unemployment	70%
Corruption and ineffectiveness of the Afghan Govt	48%
Taliban	36%
Other countries	25%
Al Qaeda	18%
Presence of international forces	18%
Lack of support from the international community	17%
Warlords	15%
Criminal groups	14%
Other reasons	2%

Note that multiple responses were permitted; figures not cumulative.

TAKEN FROM: *The Cost of War: Afghan Experiences of Conflict*, November 2009, p. 23. http://www.oxfamamerica.org/files/the-cost-of-war.pdf.

Politically and economically, Afghanistan is in collapse. Additional troops, redeployed from Iraq, have little to safeguard as the country's infrastructure continues to rot. At the local level, the Afghan—whether a shopkeeper, doctor, farmer, governor, teacher, judge, imam, taxi driver, policeman or other civil servant—must be equipped with the financial and technical means for basic survival.

After being siphoned off by handlers from Washington to Kabul, American aid flows feebly on the ground, making it nearly impossible for the average Afghan to see visible improvement. Without tangible benefits in a country struggling with over 40% [un]employment, 28% literacy and two-thirds living on less than $2 a day, the formation of alternative allegiances outside government auspices is hardly surprising.

The infamous Helmand province, for example, has upwards of 80% unemployment in places, with two poorly stocked hospitals supplying healthcare for over 700,000 persons, and it remains the nation's hottest province in terms of Taliban activity and poppy production. Illicit political and economic operations flowering in the country's poorest province is hardly coincidental when Kabul is utterly uncompetitive.

The best salve, then, for this seven-year burn, treats the fragile, fertile ground that foments violence. Saudi's hand, if extended to the Taliban, will undoubtedly be directed toward this goal. If manoeuvred deftly, King Abdullah provides the tribal Pashtuns (rallied under the Taliban) a much needed voice in long-unrepresented Kabul, secures an ally in cooling Pakistan's border, and creates a pretext for holding culpable Mecca's negotiators.

Meanwhile, America's hand, if played in the pursuit of political and economic solutions, begins to build the basis of a country worth living, not dying, for.

Periodical Bibliography

The following articles have been selected to supplement the diverse views presented in this chapter.

Al Arabiya News Channel	"Karzai Visits Saudi Arabia in Taliban 'Peace Bid,'" February 2, 2010.
Miles Amoore	"Iranians Train Taliban to Use Roadside Bombs," TimesOnline.com, March 21, 2010.
Greg Bruno	"Iran and the Future of Afghanistan," *Council on Foreign Relations*, March 30, 2009.
George Garner	"The Afghan Taliban and Pakistan's 'Strategic Depth,'" *Bellum*, May 17, 2010.
Huda al Husseini	"Will The Taliban Take Over Pashtun Areas of Afghanistan?" *Asharq Alawsat*, February 27, 2009.
Peter Lee	"Taliban Force a China Switch," *Asia Times*, March 6, 2009.
Radio Free Europe/Radio Liberty	"Russia Open to Moderate Taliban Contacts," March 25, 2009.
Beena Sarwar	"Pakistan/India: Taliban as Common Enemy," *IPS*, February 17, 2009.
Strategy Page	"Counter-Terrorism: China Versus the Taliban," August 14, 2007.

For Further Discussion

Chapter 1

1. Read over the viewpoints by Mili and Carpenter. Based on these essays, do you think defeating the Taliban would radically alter the culture of Afghanistan? Would drugs still be serious problems in a post-Taliban Afghanistan?

Chapter 2

1. Barack Obama and John Mueller agree that the war in Iraq was unnecessary. On what basis then do they disagree about the war in Afghanistan?

2. Do Inge Fryklund and Peter Bergen believe that the Taliban are popular in Afghanistan? How does this shape their policy recommendations?

Chapter 3

1. Husain Haqqani says the United States is not giving Pakistan the military equipment it needs. Based on Selig S. Harrison's essay, why might the United States be reluctant to provide Pakistan with all the military equipment it requests?

2. Pratap Chatterjee argues that war may destabilize Pakistan. What does Shuja Nawaz offer as an alternate approach to dealing with the Taliban? Do you think Nawaz's approach effectively would mean capitulating to the Taliban similar to the manner described by Susanne Koelbl?

Chapter 4

1. According to STRATFOR and Dmitry Shlapentokh, do the governments of Iran, Russia, and China all want the

United States to fail in its efforts to contain the Taliban? Is this perspective contradicted in the viewpoints of Ron Synovitz and Ryan Mauro, which suggest that individuals in Iran and Russia are supplying the Taliban with weapons?

2. Rachel Ehrenfeld notes that Saudi Arabia holds telethons to support Palestinians wounded in conflicts with Israel, but does not hold give enough support to those in Pakistan wounded or displaced by the Taliban. She concludes that this is an "indirect endorsement" by the Saudis of the Taliban. Is this argument convincing? Does she provide any other evidence that the Saudi government supports the Taliban?

Organizations to Contact

The editors have compiled the following list of organizations concerned with the issues debated in this book. The descriptions are derived from materials provided by the organizations. All have publications or information available for interested readers. The list was compiled on the date of publication of the present volume; the information provided here may change. Be aware that many organizations take several weeks or longer to respond to inquiries, so allow as much time as possible.

Afghan Red Crescent Society
Sera Meyasht Ave.,
Kabul Afghanistan
0093 75 202 36 31 • fax: 0093 75 202 34 76
e-mail: int.relation.arcs@gmail.com
Web site: www.arcs.org.af

The International Federation of Red Cross and Red Crescent Societies is the world's largest humanitarian organization, providing relief assistance around the world. The Red Crescent is used in place of the Red Cross in many Islamic countries. The group's mission is to improve the lives of vulnerable people, especially those who are victims of natural disasters, poverty, wars, and health emergencies. The Afghan Red Crescent Society's Web site provides specific information about the group's activities in Afghanistan.

Afghanistan Relief Organization (ARO)
PO Box 866, Cypress, CA 90630
(877) 276-2440 • fax: (714) 661-5932
Web site: www.afghanrelief.org

The Afghanistan Relief Organization is a humanitarian organization established in 1997 in response to the economic and physical hardships suffered by the Afghan people after decades of war. It is a volunteer organization funded by public donations that provides relief supplies and runs several health, literacy, and other programs to help the poor in Afghanistan. The ARO Web site contains an overview of Afghanistan, materials teachers can use to educate students about Afghanistan, and links to newsletters discussing ARO news and activities.

Human Rights Watch (HRW)
350 Fifth Ave., 34th Floor, New York, NY   10118-3299
(212) 290-4700 • fax: (212) 736-1300
e-mail: hrwnyc@hrw.org
Web site: www.hrw.org

Human Rights Watch is an independent organization dedicated to defending and protecting human rights around the world. It seeks to focus international attention on places where human rights are violated, give voice to the oppressed, and hold oppressors accountable for their crimes. The HRW Web site includes numerous reports on human rights in Afghanistan, including "Afghanistan: Return of the Warlords" and "Afghanistan: U.S. Investigation of Airstrike Deaths 'Deeply Flawed.'"

Institute for Afghan Studies (IAS)
e-mail: info@institute-for-afghan-studies.org
Web site: www.institute-for-afghan-studies.org

Funded and run by young Afghan scholars from around the world, the Institute for Afghan Studies seeks to promote a better understanding of Afghanistan through scholarly research and studies. The IAS Web site provides a wealth of information on the history and politics of Afghanistan, including weekly political analyses, reports and articles, and biographical information about key political figures in Afghanistan. Examples of publications include "One Scary Voter Registration at a Time" and "Afghan Economy in the War and Pre-War Period."

Islamic Republic of Afghanistan/Office of the President
0093 (0) 202 141 135

e-mail: akariobi@gmail.com
Web site: www.president.gov.af

This central Web site of the Afghanistan government provides information about Afghanistan's president, National Assembly, constitution, cabinet, departments, and commissions. It contains news reports, presidential speeches and decrees, press releases and statements, as well as links to other government-affiliated Web sites.

NATO in Afghanistan

Blvd. Leopold III, Brussels   1110
Belgium
e-mail: natodoc@hq.nato.int
Web site: www.nato.int/cps/en/natolive/topics_8189.htm

NATO in Afghanistan is part of the North Atlantic Treaty Organization (NATO), an alliance of 26 countries from Europe and North America committed to fulfilling the joint security goals of the 1949 North Atlantic Treaty. The Afghanistan section of the Web site provides an overview of NATO's interests and mission in Afghanistan and includes a link to the International Security Assistance Force (ISAF), a NATO military force that provides security, reconstruction, and development support to the Afghan government. The Web site includes documents and press releases, such as "Statement by the NATO Secretary General on the Nomination of the New Afghan Government."

Revolutionary Association of the Women of Afghanistan (RAWA)

PO Box 374,
Quetta Pakistan
0092-300-5541258 • fax: 0044-870-8312326
e-mail: rawa@rawa.org
Web site: www.rawa.org

The Revolutionary Association of the Women of Afghanistan was established in Kabul, Afghanistan, in 1977 as an independent political/social organization of Afghan women fighting for peace, freedom, and democracy in Afghanistan. The founders were several female Afghan intellectuals, and RAWA's objective was to involve Afghan women in acquiring women's human rights and establishing an Afghan government based on democratic and secular values. RAWA also solicits public donations for relief aid and projects to assist schools, orphanages, and women's cooperatives. RAWA's Web site includes press statements and speeches, as well as links to news, reports, and articles about political, social, and economic issues in Afghanistan. Recent publications include "An Overview on the Situation of Afghan Women" and "Some of the Restrictions Imposed by Taliban on Women."

United Nations Development Programme (UNDP)
1 United Nations Plaza, New York, NY   10017
(212) 906-5000 • fax: (212) 906-5001
e-mail: publications.queries@undp.org
Web site: www.undp.org

The United Nations Development Programme is an organization created by the United Nations to promote global development and help connect developing countries to knowledge, experience and resources to help their people build a better life. Among other activities, the UNDP coordinates efforts to reach the Millenium Development Goals, a commitment by world leaders to cut world poverty in half by 2015. The Web site includes a number of relevant publications, including "Fast Facts: UNDP in Afghanistan," and "Afghanistan: Disbandment of Illegal Armed Groups."

U.S. Department of State
2201 C St. NW, Washington, DC   20520
(202) 647-4000
Web site: www.state.gov

The U.S. Department of State is a federal agency that advises the president on issues of foreign policy. Its Web site includes a section on "Countries" that provides a great deal of information about Afghanistan, including an overview of the nation and materials relating to reconstruction, U.S. aid, and NATO's involvement in the country. Publications available through the Web site include "U.S. Forces in Afghanistan," and "NATO in Afghanistan: A Test of the Transatlantic Alliance."

U.S.–Afghan Women's Council
Georgetown University Center for Child and Human Development, Washington, DC   20057
(202) 687-5095 • fax: (202) 687-1954
e-mail: ew245@georgetown.edu
Web site: http://gucchd.georgetown.edu/76315.html

The U.S.–Afghan Women's Council, a project of the U.S. State Department, was created to promote private/public partnerships between U.S. and Afghan institutions and to mobilize private resources to help Afghan women gain skills and education and play a role in the reconstruction of Afghanistan. The council is now associated with Georgetown University. The Web site includes the organization's newsletter, *Connections*, as well as news, speeches, fact sheets, press releases, and information about projects affecting Afghan women.

Bibliography of Books

Sarah Chayes   *The Punishment of Virtue: Inside Afghanistan After the Taliban.* New York: Penguin Press, 2007.

Steve Coil   *Ghost Wars: The Secret History of the CIA, Afghanistan, and Bin Laden, from the Soviet Invasion to September 10, 2001.* New York: Penguin Books, 2004.

Robert D. Crews and Amin Tarzi, eds.   *The Taliban and the Crisis of Afghanistan.* Cambridge, MA: Harvard University Press, 2008.

Gregory Feifer   *The Great Gamble: The Soviet War in Afghanistan.* New York: HarperCollins, 2009.

Paul Fitzgerald and Elizabeth Gould   *Invisible History: Afghanistan's Untold Story.* San Francisco: City Lights Publisher, 2009.

Antonio Giustozzi   *Koran, Kalashnikov, and Laptop: The Neo-Taliban Insurgency in Afghanistan.* New York: Columbia University Press, 2008.

Joel Hafvenstein   *Opium Season: A Year on the Afghan Frontier.* Guilford, CT: Lyons Press, 2007.

Hussain Haqqani   *Pakistan: Between Mosque and Military.* Washington, DC: Carnegie Endowment for International Peace, 2005.

Zahid Hussain

Frontline Pakistan: The Struggle with Militant Islam. New York: Columbia University Press, 2008.

Seth G. Jones

In the Graveyard of Empires: America's War in Afghanistan. New York: W.W. Norton & Company, 2009.

Sonali Kolhatkar and James Ingalls

Bleeding Afghanistan: Washington, Warlords, and the Propaganda of Silence. New York: Seven Stories Press, 2006.

David Loyn

In Afghanistan: Two Hundred Years of British, Russian and American Occupation. New York: Palgrave MacMillan, 2009.

David Macdonald

Drugs in Afghanistan: Opium, Outlaws, and Scorpion Tales. Ann Arbor, MI: Pluto Press, 2007.

A. Manzar

Taliban in Pakistan: A Chronicle of Resurgence. Hauppauge, NY: Nova Science, 2010.

David Mares

Drug Wars and Coffeehouses: The Political Economy of the International Drug Trade. Washington, DC: CQ Press, 2006.

Nick B. Mills

Karzai: The Failing American Intervention and the Struggle for Afghanistan. Hoboken, NJ: John Wiley & Sons, 2007.

Matthew J. Morgan
A Democracy Is Born: An Insider's Account of the Battle Against Terrorism in Afghanistan. Westport, CT: Greenwood Publishing Group, 2007.

Leigh Neville
Special Operations Forces in Afghanistan: Afghanistan 2001–2007. Oxford, England: Osprey Publishing, 2008.

Gretchen Peters
Seeds of Terror: How Heroin Is Bankrolling the Taliban and al Qaeda. New York: Thomas Dunne Books, 2009.

Ahmed Rashid
Taliban: Islam, Oil and the New Great Game in Central Asia. New York: I.B. Tauris & Co., 2008.

Ahmed Rashid
Descent into Chaos: The U.S. and the Disaster in Pakistan, Afghanistan, and Central Asia. New York: Penguin Group, 2009.

Ahmed Rashid
Taliban: Militant Islam, Oil and Fundamentalism in Central Asia, 2nd ed. New Haven, CT: Yale University Press, 2010.

Robert I. Rotberg, ed.
Corruption, Global Security, and World Order. Cambridge, MA: World Peace Foundation, 2009.

Barnett R. Rubin
Afghanistan's Uncertain Transition from Turmoil to Normalcy. New York: Council on Foreign Relations, 2006.

Stephen Tanner   *Afghanistan: A Military History from Alexander the Great to the War Against the Taliban.* Philadelphia: Da Capo Press, 2009.

Abdul Salam Zaeef   *My Life with the Taliban.* New York: Columbia University Press, 2010.

Mariam Abou Zahab   *Islamist Networks: The Afghan-Pakistan Connection.* New York: Columbia University Press, 2007.

Index